CRATER LAKE & BEYOND

THE LAND OF FIRE AND ICE

JIM TURNER

WITH PHOTOGRAPHS BY
Jay and Sue Newman

RIO NUEVO
PUBLISHERS

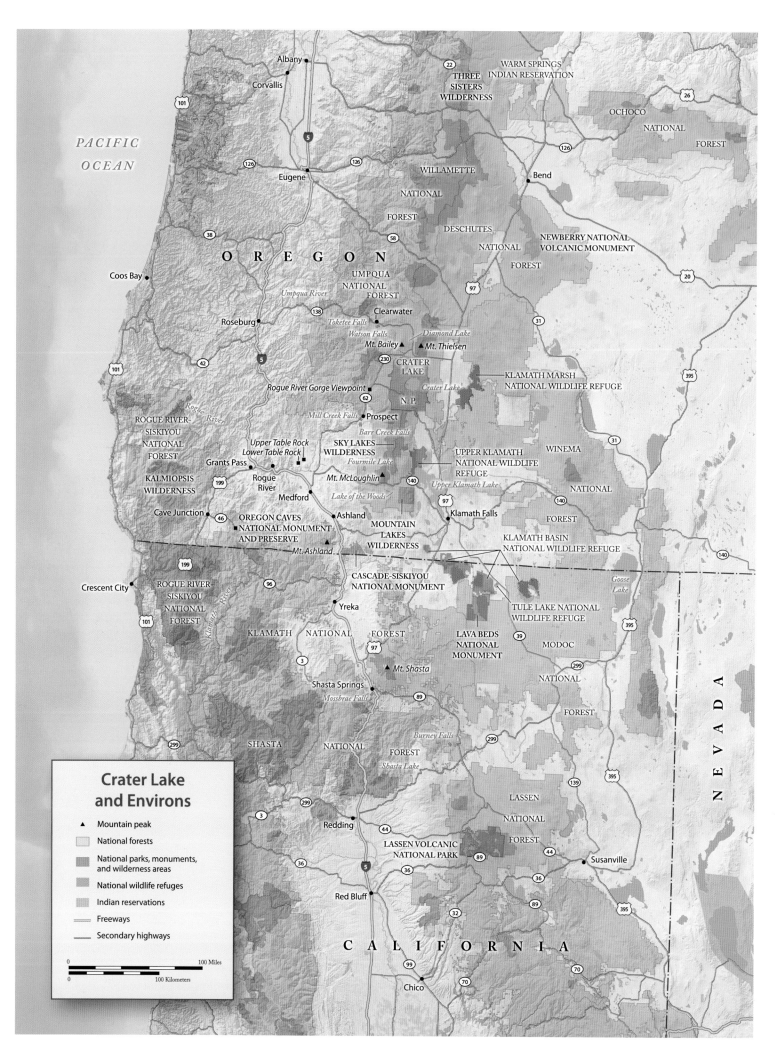

PACIFIC
OCEAN

Albany

Corvallis

101

126

Eugene

126

126

5

22

THREE
SISTERS
WILDERNESS

WARM SPRINGS
INDIAN RESERVATION

26

OCHOCO

NATIONAL

FOREST

WILLAMETTE

NATIONAL

FOREST

Bend

126

DESCHUTES

NATIONAL

FOREST

NEWBERRY NATIONAL
VOLCANIC MONUMENT

20

O R E G O N

58

Coos Bay

38

UMPQUA
NATIONAL
FOREST

Umpqua River

Roseburg

138

Toketee Falls

Watson Falls

Clearwater

Diamond Lake

Mt. Bailey ▲

97

31

▲ Mt. Thielsen

395

42

5

230

CRATER
LAKE

Crater Lake

KLAMATH MARSH
NATIONAL WILDLIFE REFUGE

101

Rogue River Gorge Viewpoint

62

N.P.

Rogue River

Mill Creek Falls

Prospect

Barr Creek Falls

31

ROGUE RIVER-
SISKIYOU

NATIONAL

FOREST

Upper Table Rock
Lower Table Rock

SKY LAKES
WILDERNESS

Fourmile Lake

WINEMA

KALMIOPSIS
WILDERNESS

Grants Pass

199

Rogue
River

▲ Mt. McLoughlin

140

UPPER KLAMATH
NATIONAL WILDLIFE
REFUGE

Upper Klamath Lake

NATIONAL

140

Medford

Lake of the Woods

97

Cave Junction

46

OREGON CAVES
NATIONAL MONUMENT
AND PRESERVE

Ashland

MOUNTAIN
LAKES
WILDERNESS

Klamath Falls

FOREST

Mt. Ashland

KLAMATH BASIN
NATIONAL WILDLIFE REFUGE

140

199

CASCADE-SISKIYOU
NATIONAL MONUMENT

Goose
Lake

Crescent City

ROGUE RIVER-
SISKIYOU

NATIONAL

FOREST

96

Yreka

TULE LAKE NATIONAL
WILDLIFE REFUGE

395

101

Klamath River

KLAMATH

NATIONAL

FOREST

97

39

LAVA BEDS
NATIONAL
MONUMENT

MODOC

299

3

NATIONAL

▲ Mt. Shasta

Shasta Springs

Mossbrae Fall

89

FOREST

299

Burney Falls

299

SHASTA

NATIONAL

FOREST

Shasta Lake

139

395

LASSEN

NATIONAL

299

3

Redding

44

FOREST

44

Susanville

36

LASSEN VOLCANIC
NATIONAL PARK

89

44

36

36

89

Red Bluff

32

C A L I F O R N I A

99

70

70

Chico

N E V A D A

Crater Lake
and Environs

▲ Mountain peak

National forests

National parks, monuments,
and wilderness areas

National wildlife refuges

Indian reservations

Freeways

Secondary highways

0   100 Miles

0   100 Kilometers

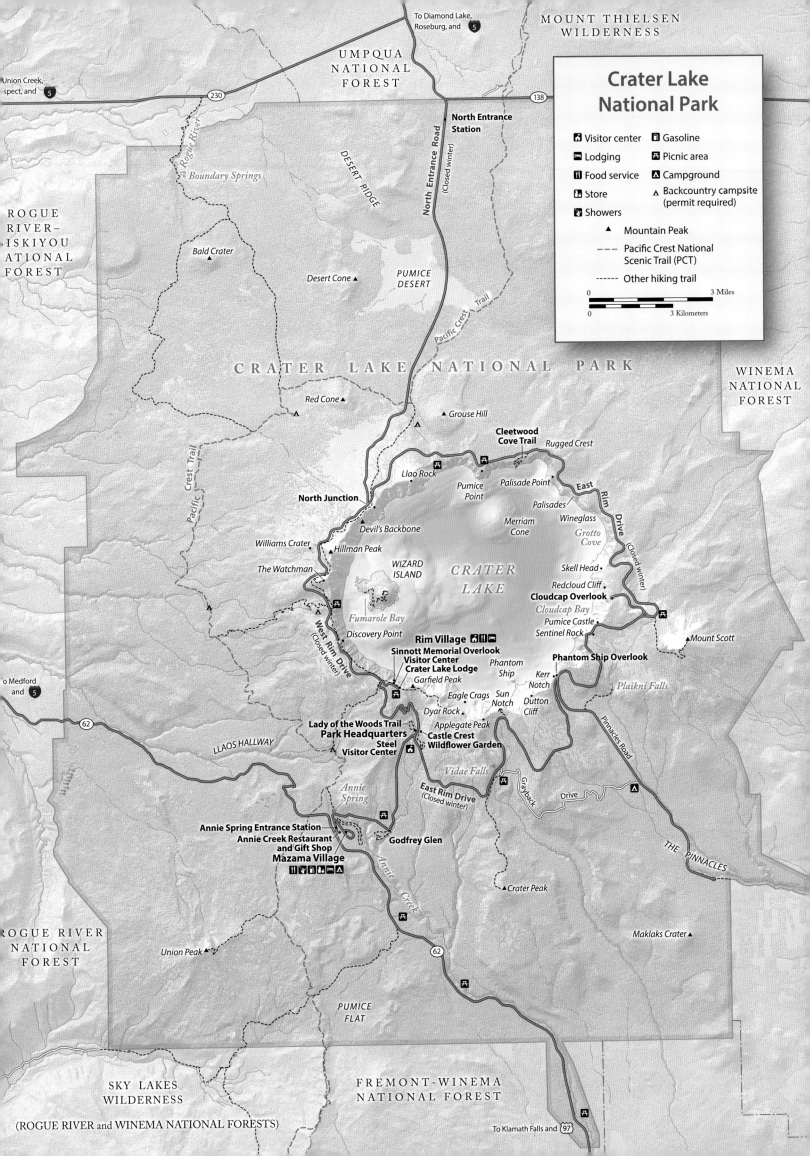

Crater Lake National Park

- 🏛 Visitor center
- 🏨 Lodging
- 🍴 Food service
- 🏪 Store
- 🚿 Showers
- ⛽ Gasoline
- ⛱ Picnic area
- ⛺ Campground
- ▲ Backcountry campsite (permit required)
- ▲ Mountain Peak
- --- Pacific Crest National Scenic Trail (PCT)
- ···· Other hiking trail

0 ——————— 3 Miles
0 ——————— 3 Kilometers

MOUNT THIELSEN WILDERNESS

To Diamond Lake, Roseburg, and 5

UMPQUA NATIONAL FOREST

Union Creek, spect, and 5

230

ROGUE RIVER–ISKIYOU NATIONAL FOREST

Boundary Springs

Rogue River

Bald Crater ▲

Desert Cone ▲

DESERT RIDGE

PUMICE DESERT

North Entrance Road (Closed winter)

138

North Entrance Station

Pacific Crest Trail

CRATER LAKE NATIONAL PARK

WINEMA NATIONAL FOREST

Red Cone ▲

Grouse Hill ▲

Cleetwood Cove Trail

Rugged Crest

Llao Rock

Pumice Point

Palisade Point

East

Palisades

Wineglass

North Junction

Merriam Cone

Grotto Cove

Rim Drive (Closed winter)

Devil's Backbone

Williams Crater

Hillman Peak ▲

Skell Head

Redcloud Cliff

Cloudcap Overlook

The Watchman

WIZARD ISLAND

CRATER LAKE

Cloudcap Bay

Pumice Castle

Sentinel Rock

Pacific Crest Trail

West Rim Drive (Closed winter)

Fumarole Bay

Discovery Point

Rim Village 🏛🍴

Mount Scott ▲

o Medford and 5

62

Sinnott Memorial Overlook
Visitor Center
Crater Lake Lodge

Phantom Ship

Phantom Ship Overlook

Plaikni Falls

Garfield Peak

Kerr Notch

Eagle Crags

Sun Notch

Dyar Rock

Dutton Cliff

Lady of the Woods Trail
Park Headquarters
Steel Visitor Center

Applegate Peak

Castle Crest Wildflower Garden

LLAOS HALLWAY

Vidae Falls

Annie Spring

East Rim Drive (Closed winter)

Pinnacles Road

Grayback Drive

Annie Spring Entrance Station
Annie Creek Restaurant and Gift Shop
Mazama Village
🍴🚿🏪🍴⛽⛺

Godfrey Glen

Annie Creek

THE PINNACLES

Crater Peak ▲

ROGUE RIVER NATIONAL FOREST

Union Peak ▲

PUMICE FLAT

Maklaks Crater ▲

SKY LAKES WILDERNESS

FREMONT-WINEMA NATIONAL FOREST

(ROGUE RIVER and WINEMA NATIONAL FORESTS)

62

To Klamath Falls and 97

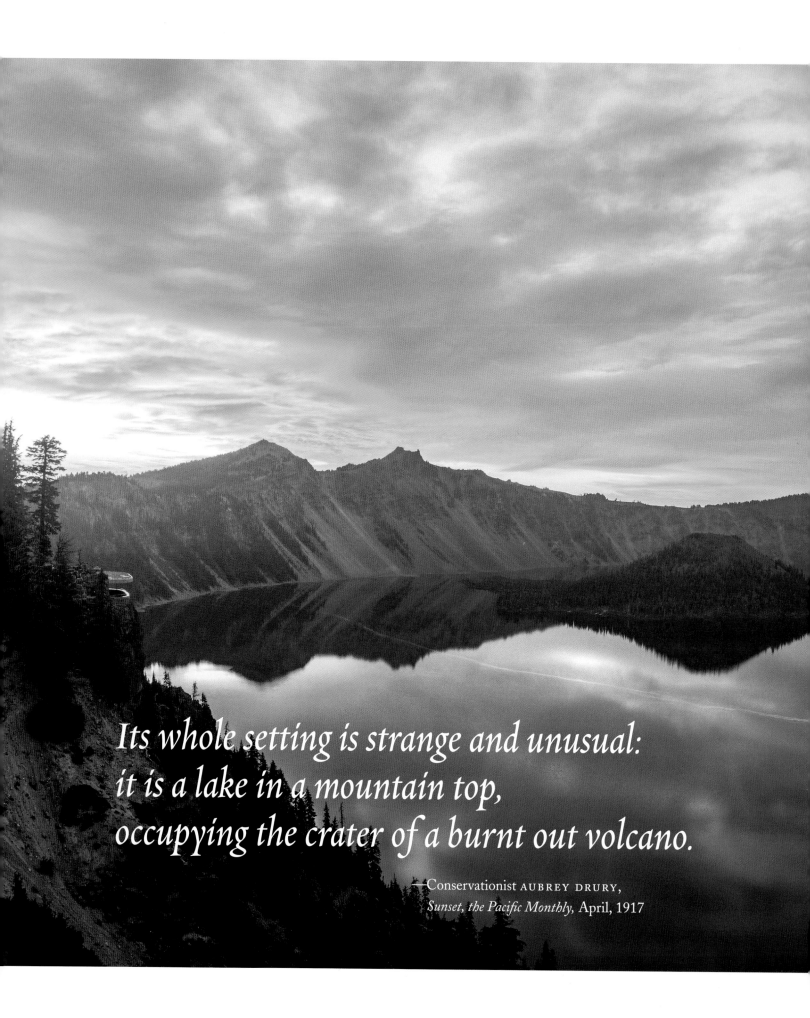

Its whole setting is strange and unusual:
it is a lake in a mountain top,
occupying the crater of a burnt out volcano.

—Conservationist AUBREY DRURY,
Sunset, the Pacific Monthly, April, 1917

N A CALM, CLEAR DAY, Crater Lake seems like an illusion, nature's giant mirror trick. Where does the sky end and the lake begin? It boggles the mind with pleasant wonder. Lakes have formed in volcanic calderas (bowl-shaped basins formed by eruptions that cause volcanic mountains to collapse in on themselves) all over the world, as far flung as Ecuador, Indonesia, and several African countries, and most people agree that Crater Lake is the finest example of this phenomenon.

Growing out of the pumice: Wild buckwheat blooms beneath a clump of rabbit brush.

LEFT: *The first view of Crater Lake and Wizard Island that most visitors see is this one from Rim Village.*

Clean, Serene, and Ultramarine

About 7,700 years ago Mount Mazama erupted and its walls collapsed, leaving a bowl-shaped caldera 2,148 feet deep (655 m) where the top of the mountain used to be. Crater Lake is six miles long, five miles wide, and 1,943 feet (592 meters) deep. It is the deepest lake in the United States and considered by most geographers to be the ninth deepest lake in the world and one of the five clearest lakes on Earth.

Snow and rain created a lake so clear that you can see more than 144 feet down on a sunny, calm day. No rivers flow into or out of the lake, and rain and snowfall offset evaporation and seepage to keep it very close to the same volume and depth constantly. Experts estimate that the water is completely replaced about every 250 years. There are few fish or other pollutants, so the water is quite pure.

American Indian legend says that the bluebird was gray until it dipped itself in Crater Lake. Because of its breathtaking sapphire blue waters, Oregon pioneers began petitioning to make the Crater Lake area a national park in the 1870s and they were rewarded for their efforts in 1902, making it the fifth oldest national park in the United States.

More than seven thousand years ago, Mount Mazama spewed clouds of ash, cinders, and pumice thirty miles into the air, as portrayed in this painting by Paul Rockwood.

OPPOSITE TOP: *A golden-mantled ground squirrel pauses to get a better look.*

OPPOSITE BOTTOM: *Wizard Island offers hikers two trails: one to the summit, and this shorter one to Fumarole Bay. Hillman Peak rises in the background.*

Mount Mazama is part of the Cascade Volcanic Arc, the largest collection of volcanoes in North America, stretching from northern California, up through Oregon and Washington, and into British Columbia in southwest Canada. In addition, the area surrounding this lake in the volcano has other features to recommend it.

In addition to Crater Lake, southern Oregon and northern California have many wonders to describe. There are three untamed rivers teeming with salmon and trout, where rafting and kayaking adventures abound. The area contains several more volcanic areas, including Newberry National Volcanic Monument, Lava Beds National Monument, Oregon Caves, California's Mount Lassen and the imposing Mount Shasta. In these places and other areas, you will see prehistoric sites and rock art, waterfalls and wildflowers galore, and a marble cave that was home to a prehistoric grizzly bear 50,000 years ago.

Lava Fire & Icy Water

Visitors usually enter Crater Lake National Park from the south, sixty miles from Klamath Falls on Highways 97 and then 62, or from the southwest on Highway 62, about eighty-five miles from where it meets Interstate 5 at Medford, Oregon. Highway 62 and the access road to the lake are open all winter, but the scenic Rim Drive closes in the winter months because of excessive snowfall.

Crater Lake is almost circular. The magma chamber beneath the volcano was emptied and a series of volcanic fractures called a fault ring developed around the edge of the chamber. The emptied chamber couldn't support the weight of the walls around it, and the center of the volcano within the ring fracture collapsed, forming an almost circular caldera basin.

This collapse left lava cliffs around the circumference, towering as much as 1,000 feet above the surface of the lake. There are approximately twenty-one square miles, or 183,224 acres (74,148 hectares) of water in the lake.

Climate: Clear and Cold

It's not widely known, but with an annual average of more than forty feet (12 m) of snow every year, Crater Lake National Park is one of the "snowiest" places in the United States. However, the levels have

The last light of a December day kisses the tops of mountain hemlocks, the Watchman, and Hillman Peak.

RIGHT: *Some winter views are only accessible while wearing snowshoes, like this one looking west toward Rogue River National Forest.*

been getting smaller every year since records began in 1931. In 2015, the amount was 16 feet (5 m), the lowest ever.

Crater Lake rarely freezes because weather systems begin over the relatively warm Pacific Ocean, 115 miles to the west. The heavy snowfall is caused by the "lake effect," which occurs when a mass of cold air moves across a body of warmer lake (or ocean) water. The lower layer of air picks up water vapor and rises up into the colder air, freezes, and creates heavy snows inland. This process is enhanced when the air rises up into mountains, which produces narrow bands of intense snowfall. Since the elevation of Medford, Oregon, less than eighty miles from the lake is 1,382 feet (421 m), and Crater Lake is almost five thousand feet higher, the rapid change in elevation is a major cause of the heavy snow.

Subnivean (in and underneath the snowpack) animals, such as pikas, voles, and shrews, live under the protective heavy snow layers. But more important, the melting snow furnishes water to the southern part of the state via the Klamath, Rogue, and Umpqua Rivers, providing sustenance not only to city dwellers but also farmers, ranchers, and local wildlife.

In March, the typical snow depth at Crater Lake headquarters has been eleven feet, but in 2015 it was three feet, the lowest amount for that date in recorded history. But in December, Crater Lake broke the record for the largest snowfall in that month. The National Weather Service reported that 196.7 inches fell that month, compared to the previous record of 196 inches in 1948. The National Park Service reported that the annual amount of snowfall has decreased gradually over the past eight decades from 614 inches in the 1930s to 474 inches in 2013. The numbers rose in some decades in between, but the trend for the last decade has been a steady decline that scientists expect to continue indefinitely. Lower snow levels can lead to more forest fires, more insects, and draught difficulties for local plants and animals.

High winds blew the snow to the north side of this tree, keeping the winter sun from melting it.

LEFT: *Wildlife is sparse on the crater rim during the winter months, but deer still feed at the lower elevations.*

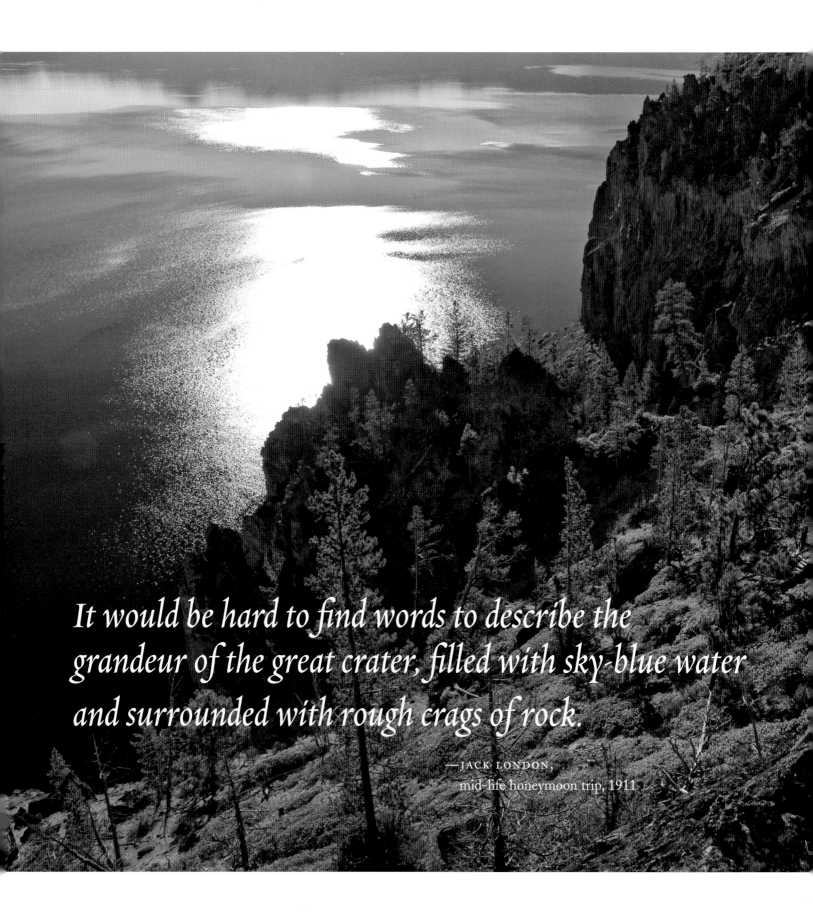

It would be hard to find words to describe the grandeur of the great crater, filled with sky-blue water and surrounded with rough crags of rock.

—JACK LONDON,
mid-life honeymoon trip, 1911

8

Crater Lake Geology

The Mount Mazama volcano that created Crater Lake is not an isolated phenomenon, but a part of the world's largest violent geological activity area, the Pacific Ring of Fire. Crater Lake lies within one of the most active parts of that ring, the Cascades Volcanic Arc. The Pacific Ring of Fire is more like a 25,000-mile horseshoe shape than a ring. It is a string of volcanoes and seismic activity sites around the Pacific Ocean's shores, a band that is sometimes hundreds of miles wide. If you look at a map of the Pacific Ocean and start at your lower left, the ring extends from New Zealand north to New Guinea and up the Asian Coast through the Philippines, Japan, and the Kurile Islands, up to the Alaskan Aleutians, then down the North American west coast and on down almost to the tip of South America. Several Antarctic volcanoes, dormant and active, "close the ring."

According to the National Geographic Encyclopedia, the ring contains 75% of the earth's active volcanoes, and 90% of all earthquakes occur along the Ring of Fire. The ring is caused by the movement of huge slabs of the earth's crust called tectonic plates. Imagine that these plates are like pieces of a piecrust, fitting together like a jigsaw puzzle, floating on the warmer, more fluid underlying molten rock called the mantle. When the tectonic plates collide over eons of time, they slide under and over each other, causing earthquakes, faults, and volcanic activity. These are called active zones, and more occur in the Ring of Fire than anywhere else in the world. When the edge of one plate crashes into the boundaries of other plates, the heavier plate slides under the lighter one, which creates a deep underwater trench. This process is called subduction, and it changes the ordinarily dense mantle into a more buoyant and fluid magma, which pushes its way up to, and through, the earth's crust.

The evening sun lights up the forest, rocks, and water below Palisade Point on the north rim.

RIGHT: *Crater Lake's volcanic neighbors to the north: Middle Sister, North Sister, and Broken Top.*

9

Of the fifteen to twenty ever-changing rigid but brittle tectonic plates, the Juan de Fuca Plate, often called a microplate because of its size, is the primary cause of earthquakes and volcanism from northwest California to southwest Canada. It is a remnant of the former huge Farallon Plate, which subducted underneath the North American Plate during the Jurassic period. According to the Pacific Northwest Seismic Network, the small Juan de Fuca Plate is moving to the east-northeast at about 1.6 inches a year. Its motion is sticky rather than smooth, however. Pressure builds up until the fault breaks and a dozen feet of the microplate slide under North America by means of large earthquakes. These openings in the earth's crust allow molten rock from the earth's mantle to flow to the surface, or form chains of mountains and volcanoes. From thirty-seven to two million years ago, the Juan de Fuca Plate subduction created a line of active volcanoes known as a volcanic arc.

In the Cascade Mountain Range in the Pacific Northwest, there are more than twenty major volcanoes and more than four thousand separate volcanic vents. This Cascade Volcanic Arc reaches from southwestern British Columbia south through Washington, Oregon, and northern California. Twelve of the volcanoes are more than 10,000 feet high (3,000 m) and both Mount Rainier and Mount Shasta are more than 14,000 feet high (4,300 m). Mount Mazama, (once 12,000 feet high or 3,657 meters), the volcano that created Crater Lake, is part of this arc.

BELOW: *Mighty Mount Shasta, 100 miles to the south in California, is so high that its peak can be seen from Crater Lake on a clear day.*

OPPOSITE TOP: *Clouds engulf Mount Bailey, allowing the lesser-known Bald Crater in the northwest corner of the park to steal the spotlight.*

A Clark's nutcracker keeps watch on an interpretive sign.

The What, Why, and How of Volcanoes

Generally, as one tectonic plate rams into another and slides underneath it, friction creates heat as they grind together, melting solid rock from the planet's mantle or crust into pressurized magma (liquid rock) reservoirs.

These pools remain underground for thousands of years under increasing pressure from surrounding rocks and the hot molten magma is pushed upward until it melts a channel in fractured rock and blasts a hole in the earth's surface, or erupts through cracks formed by earthquakes, also created by the colliding tectonic plates.

Hot gases, lava, pumice, cinders, and rock fragments blast out of a central vent, spewing this volcanic matter as much as thirty miles into the air. The heavier materials fall back down and pile up around the vent and form a volcano. When the primary eruption ends, a bowl-shaped crater forms inside the top of the volcano. The vent, usually plugged by cooled, hardened lava, lies at the bottom of the crater.

Calderas, vents, plates—volcanoes have a language all their own. The names stem from ancient Greek and, more specifically, from their god of fire, Vulcan, who was associated with metal forges, blacksmithing, and volcanoes. Over the centuries, scientists have added many more words. Since Crater Lake is the product of a volcano, a few definitions are in order here. For some reason no one can explain with any logic, molten rock and metal in the mantle (the layer below the earth's crust), is called magma, but as soon as this same material reaches the surface through gas pressure, cracks, and vents, its name changes immediately to lava.

The major type of rock associated with volcanoes is basalt. Basalt is a dark, fine-grained igneous rock (magma solidified through the volcanic process) that makes up most of the earth's bedrock. It erupts at a higher temperature and contains more iron and less silicon than other types of lava. This combination makes basalt very fluid. It can go down the sides of volcanoes at speeds up to one hundred miles an hour, traveling up to forty miles before it cools down to hard black rock.

Andesite is also an igneous rock, but it erupts at cooler temperatures and contains more silica and less iron. That makes it flow slower in thicker clumps that don't travel as far. Geologists coined the scientific term "stickier" to describe this characteristic.

Rhyolite, another form of volcanic rock with a high silica content, has gas bubbles trapped inside it that explode when it reaches the surface, hurling "frothy bits" (another jot of enjoyable geologist jargon) of lava high into the sky. Rhyolite sometimes cools almost instantly into bubble-filled, light-as-a-feather glass.

If rhyolite oozes out of a volcanic vent like toothpaste, it cools almost instantly, forming obsidian. This is a dark, often transparent glass that shatters into sharp shards when struck. It was prized by Native peoples for its suitability for cutting tools and spear points.

Red and black cinders are formed when molten gas-filled lava is shot into the air, bursts into small particles, and hardens as it falls to Earth. Pumice (a porous form of volcanic glass) is formed the same way, except that it is created from denser basalt and andesite lavas that contain more magnesium and iron.

From Sentinel Rock, looking west across the lake, Watchman Peak is more than five miles away.

Mount Mazama

In 1896, a Portland mountain climbing club called The Mazamas took a trip to Crater Lake and they named the mountain after their club. The hikers thought the term was a Native American word meaning "mountain goat," but it is actually a Spanish word for a genus of South American deer. According to their club records, the Mazama Club was formed when 155 men and 38 women climbed Mount Hood, Oregon, on July 19, 1894. In order to become a member, climbers had to reach the top of a mountain that had at least one glacier and that could only be reached on foot. Oregon has plenty of those mountains to choose from, especially in the Cascade Volcanic Arc.

More than 400,000 years ago, volcanic eruptions in the area created Mount Scott to the east of what is now Crater Lake. Then over hundreds

The view east from Crater Lake Lodge showcases the craggy rocks of Garfield Peak in the foreground, and snowcapped Mount Scott in the background.

of thousands of years it and other volcanoes around it became extinct and new volcanoes grew to the west where Garfield and Applegate peaks are now. Mazama began to grow about 30,000 years ago, and Redcloud Cliff and Grouse Hill near the lake grew from these thick lava flows.

Mount Mazama rose 12,000 feet high (3,700 m). This strato-volcano, or composite volcano, was built up of layers of hardened volcanic materials from previous volcanoes. Stratovolcanoes have a steep profile and periodic explosive eruptions, often from several different vents. An eruption 7,900 years ago created a layer of white ash and pumice, and lava flows on top of that formed Llao Rock. Finally, about 7,700 years ago the largest explosion in the Cascades in a million years took place where Crater Lake is now.

Pressurized magma trapped about three miles (4.82 km) below the mountain's surface exploded from a vent on the northeast side of Mount Mazama near what is now called Cleetwood Cove. A giant pillar of ash and pumice shot thirty miles up into the air and drifted as far as central Canada, a thousand miles away. Approximately 180 billion tons of magma (about 14 cubic miles or 58 cubic kilo-meters) followed, turning to molten lava containing volcanic rocks,

pumice, ash, and tuff (a combination of volcanic rubble and cinders) as it emerged from the earth. The top of the mountain collapsed, opening cracks around the peak where more lava began to flow down into the caldera and down the outside slopes of Mount Mazama, devastating valleys and plains for forty miles in all directions. It took almost 400,000 years for Mount Mazama to grow to its full height, but its collapse took only days, or perhaps even hours.

To the east and north of the volcano, at least six inches of ash blanketed 5,000 square miles (12,949 square km) of land. North of Crater Lake in the Pumice Desert, pumice and ash were fifty feet deep. How much ash are we talking about? Here's a comparison developed by the staff at Crater Lake National Park: Imagine that the eruption at Mount St. Helens produced just one tablespoon of ash. Compared to that, the larger volcano at Mount Vesuvius would produce one cup, Krakatau would produce one gallon, Mount Mazama would produce three gallons of ash, the eruption at Long Valley would produce two ten-quart buckets (18.92 L), and the volcanic explosion at Yellowstone would have produced a thirty-gallon trash can full of ash! It is estimated that the major eruption at Mount Mazama was one hundred times greater than Mount St. Helens.

Ten Deepest Lakes in the World

#	Lake	Location	Depth (ft)	Depth (m)
1	Lake Baikal	Siberia, Russia	5,387 ft	(1,642 m)
2	Lake Tanganyika	Central Africa	4,823 ft	(1,470 m)
3	Caspian Sea	Central Asia	3,363 ft	(1,025 m)
4	Lake Vostok	Antarctica	3,300 ft	(1,000 m)
5	Lake O'Higgins/ San Martín Lake	Chile & Argentina	2,742 ft	(836 m)
6	Lake Malawi	Mozambique & Malawi	2,316 ft	(706 m)
7	Issyk-Kul	Kyrgyzstan	2,192 ft	(668 m)
8	Great Slave Lake	Canada	2,015 ft	(614 m)
9	Crater Lake	Oregon, United States	1,943 ft	(593 m)
10	Lake Matano	Indonesia	1,936 ft	(590 m)

1000 FT.

2000 FT.

3000 FT.

4000 FT.

5000 FT.

CRATER 9 LAKE

A Lake Inside a Volcano

The magma chamber collapsed after the eruption, forming a caldera about 4,000 feet (1,219 m) from rim to bottom. Usually, volcanic caldera walls are jagged, partial, or are broken by chasms and fissures. Geologists coined the phrase "grew, blew, fell, and fill" to describe the actions that created Crater Lake. First Mount Mazama *grew* on top of older volcanoes, and then the ashes, gasses, and other volcanic materials *blew* out the vent on the north side. Then the sides of the mountain *fell* in to create the caldera. Once the lava cooled, the lake began to *fill* with rain and melted snow water. Mount Mazama's caldera has no breaks to let the water out. Lake formation conditions were perfect.

As soon as the caldera floor was cool enough that the water didn't turn into clouds of steam when it hit, Crater Lake began to fill from groundwater draining back into the empty space and hot springs from the remaining sides of Mount Mazama. It filled faster with these extra sources, so that it probably reached 90% capacity four hundred years after the eruption, according to Crater Lake Institute expert F. Owen Hoffman. After a 1,000-year period of drier climate, the lake reached its current size about 2,500 years after the collapse of Mount Mazama. Many centuries of annual winter storms finally filled the lake with five trillion gallons of water. Snow, rain, and water runoff from the caldera's sides contribute 34 billion gallons of water to the lake, while 18 billion gallons seep out and 16 billion gallons are lost to evaporation. This creates a near perfect equilibrium while keeping the water fresh and clear.

At 1,943 feet (593 m), Crater Lake is the deepest lake in the United States and the ninth deepest lake in the world. In the past, the deepest point in each lake has determined the ranking. However, F. Owen Hoffman of Crater Lake Institute said that when viewed by average overall depth, Crater Lake's 1,145 feet (350 m) moves it up to third deepest in the world. And, among lakes whose basins are entirely above sea level, Crater Lake is the deepest in the world.

Edward S. Curtis created this picture of a Klamath Indian in 1923. He named it "Praying to the Spirits at Crater Lake."

Prehistory and Native Peoples

Artifacts indicate that prehistoric people lived in southern Oregon before Mount Mazama's eruption 7,700 years ago. Obsidian tools, atlatls (spear throwers), and moccasins have been discovered undisturbed under layers of volcanic ash east and north of the mountain.

The Legend of Crater Lake

The war that took place between Llao, god of the underworld, and Skell, god of the sky world, ranged between Mount Shasta and Mount Mazama. According to some versions of the legend, Llao lived below Lao-Yaina (Mount Mazama). There was no lake there, but he came out of a hole to stand on top of the mountain, where his head touched the stars. He fell in love with Loha, a chief's daughter, but his ugliness disgusted her. Llao swore he would punish her people with fire.

Skell came down from the Above World to the top of Mount Shasta, and the two of them hurled red-hot rocks at each other, causing a great thundering and trembling. The sky was dark for many days, and after two Klamath medicine men jumped into the fire pit, Skell defeated Llao and sent him to the Below World forever. To make sure peace and serenity took the place of the dark pit after Mount Mazama's collapse, Skell filled it with dazzling blue water.

Klamath Indian traditions, perhaps going back to their ancestors who witnessed Mount Mazama's eruption and subsequent collapse, teach that the lake is an extremely sacred site. It is said that only the most spiritual people are allowed to go on vision quests there, and they gain even more power by performing dangerous feats, such as climbing the walls of the caldera.

Fort Rock Sandals

This sandal is one of dozens found about sixty miles from Crater Lake. It was covered in ash from Mount Mazama's big eruption and dated at around 9,000 to 10,000 years old.

Here's how we know that people were in the area when Mount Mazama erupted. University of Oregon archaeologist Luther Cressman found dozens of sandals in a cave underneath a layer of volcanic ash in 1938. His discovery was near Fort Rock, Oregon, about sixty-three miles from Mount Mazama. Made of twined sagebrush bark, the sandals have been radiocarbon dated from 10,500 to 9,300 years old, thousands of years before Mazama's giant cloud headed northeast in the direction of the cave.

The Americans Go West

Since the first Wild West novels and early silent movies, several generations of people have formed the idea that the West was settled in a steady stream from east to west. That's definitely not true. Because of high mountains, broad deserts, and seagoing explorations along the Pacific Coast, Americans settled in Oregon a lot sooner than many states to the east of them. Pioneers blazed long, arduous trails over the hundreds of miles of inhospitable terrain that separated their new homeland from the rest of the United States.

The Applegate Trail or Southern Emigrant Route

In 1805, Lewis and Clark's Corps of Discovery created what would eventually be known as the Oregon Trail. One of the most dangerous parts of their route was The Dalles, a series of treacherous rapids on the

The Ivan Applegate family, some of the area's earliest settlers, at the Mount Mazama Celebration at Crater Lake.

Columbia River. After many tragic losses of lives and goods, intrepid pioneers did something to avoid this dangerous passage. Hit by the depression of 1839, Jesse Applegate and his brothers Charles and Lindsay left their Missouri farms and joined the Great Migration of 1843 on the Oregon Trail. In those early days the trail pretty much ended at Fort Walla Walla and emigrants rode boats on the Columbia River the last 250 miles to the Willamette Valley.

Entering The Dalles on November 6, 1843, one of the brothers' flatboats got caught in a whirlpool and Jesse's nine-year-old son Edward was drowned, as was Lindsay's nine-year-old son, Warren. Lindsay vowed that as soon as they were settled he would find a better route so that other families would not suffer such losses.

In 1846, Jesse, Lindsay, and some neighbors formed the Old South Road Company. They blazed a road that started at Fort Hall in southeastern Idaho on the Humboldt Trail, went south and then west across northern Nevada and the northeast corner of California before heading north up the Willamette Valley to Oregon City, fifteen miles south of Portland.

The Applegates' route went through the Klamath Lake area and reached the Rogue River Valley that fall. In no time, hundreds of other families followed this route, and the eastern part of the road would become a road to California during the Gold Rush of 1849. Anglo/Indian relations remained relatively peaceful until the Rich Gulch gold rush of 1851 brought hordes of prospectors into the area just west of Crater Lake.

In 1855–56, the U.S. Army, along with a militia made up of settlers and prospectors, mounted the Rogue River Wars, forcing the Molala, Takelma, and Upper Umpqua Native Americans onto reservations elsewhere.

Located near Prospect, the first town to the south of Crater Lake, Mill Creek Falls plunges 173 feet into the Rogue River.

OPPOSITE: *Mill Creek flows over Pearsony Falls into the Rogue River less than an hour's drive from Rim Village.*

CRATER LAKE
1874
FIRST PHOTO TAKEN
P. BRITT, Photo

A Mule Discovers the Lake

Although some may have preceded them, the earliest authenticated record of the lake's discovery dates to June 12, 1853. A party of prospectors including John W. Hillman, a native of Albany, New York, who went to the California Gold Rush three years earlier at age seventeen, came up from California into southern Oregon looking for gold. Accompanied by Patrick McManus, Isaac Skeeters, and other Oregonians, they headed up the Rogue River Valley in search of the Lost Cabin Mine. They did not find the "lost diggings" and began to run out of food. They also got hopelessly lost, and had to climb mountain peaks to get long distance views. From the top of one peak they saw numerous lakes.

They started back down and came to the rim of a precipice where Hillman described "the bluest lake I ever saw." After their excitement subsided, they discussed the most important question of what to name the lake. They narrowed the choices to two: "Mysterious Lake" or "Deep Blue Lake." The latter was chosen, although it was sometimes called

This first ever picture of Crater Lake, taken by Peter Britt in August 1874, was a crucial part of William Gladstone Steel's campaign to turn the lake into a National Park in 1902.

Lake Mystery after that. The group went back to Jacksonville, but since there would be no newspaper for another two years, it was soon looked on as a miner's tall tale, and then forgotten entirely.

As Hillman described it fifty years later: "On the evening of the first day, while riding up a long, sloping mountain, we suddenly came in sight of water, and very much surprised, as we did not expect to see any lakes, and did not know what we had come in sight of and not until my mule stopped a few feet from the rim of Crater Lake did I look down, and if I had been riding a blind mule I firmly believe I would have ridden over the edge to death and destruction."

John Hillman had the honor of having one of the most beautiful peaks in the park named after him.

In the fall of 1862, another party of miners returning from the Rogue River Valley chanced upon the mystery lake, and this time it made the newspapers. The *Oregon Sentinel* of November 8, 1862, under the headline "Oregon's Great Curiosity" made the lake a reality by putting it in print. Yet again on Saturday, September 16, 1865, the *Oregon State Journal* in Eugene City, Oregon, went on at length about the beauty of the lake:

A mule deer pauses on the Lady of the Woods Trail.

Several of our citizens returned last week from a visit to the Great Sunken Lake, situated in the Cascade Mountains, about 75 miles northeast of Jacksonville. This lake rivals the famous Valley of Sinbad the Sailor. It is thought to average 2,000 feet down to the water all round. The walls are almost perpendicular, running down into the water and leaving no bench. The depth of the water is unknown, and its surface is smooth and unruffled, as it lies too far below the surface of the mountain that the air currents do not affect it. Its length is estimated at twelve miles, and its width at ten. There is an island in its center, having trees upon it. No living man ever has and probably never will be able to reach the water's edge. It lies still silent and mysterious in the bosom of the "everlasting hills," like a huge well scooped out by the hands of giant genii of the mountains, in the unknown ages gone by and around it the primeval forests watch and ward are keeping.

Not a foot of the land about the lake had been touched or claimed. An overmastering conviction came to me that this wonderful spot must be saved, wild and beautiful, just as it was, for all future generations, and that it was up to me to do something. I then and there had the impression that in some way, I didn't know how, the lake ought to become a National Park.

—WILLIAM GLADSTONE STEEL

The Man Behind the Park

William Gladstone Steel didn't create Crater Lake National Park single-handedly, but everyone agrees that his energy and persistence made it happen. He was born September 7, 1854, to a Scottish immigrant father and Virginia-born mother. The family moved from Kansas to Portland, Oregon, in 1872.

In the summer of 1885, Steel took a vacation from his post office supervisor job to visit Crater Lake with a hiking companion, J. M. "Johnnie" Breck. In Linkville (changed to Klamath Falls in the 1890s), the hikers met Captain Clarence Dutton, on leave from the United States Geological Survey, and Klamath Indian chief Allen David. Steel said his conversations with Captain Dutton on the rim of the lake ended in agreement that they should create a national park to save the lake from commercial exploitation.

Back in Portland, the *Oregonian* published a letter from Breck, urging support for a national park. In turn, Steel wrote to almost a thousand U.S. newspaper editors asking them to support a national park. Then Steel had Oregon publishers and postmasters circulate petitions to that same purpose. The petitions were sent to President Grover Cleveland, and Steel went to Washington, D.C., in January 1886 to talk with politicians about his dream. In February, Cleveland set aside ten townships of land (23,041 acres or 9,324 hectares) around Crater Lake from the public market, pending actions to create a national park there.

While Steel was undoubtedly the leading figure in the park's creation, one must be careful when reading his historical accounts. In his well-researched *History of Crater Lake National Park*, historian Rick Harmon said that in his later years Steel felt that others did not show enough appreciation of his role, and that to remedy this Steel "took certain liberties in representing his past." Steel began to tell of how, as a Kansas school boy in the 1870s, his mother wrapped his sandwich in a newspaper article about a wonderful lake in Oregon. Harmon said that the odds of an article appearing in a Kansas paper at that time are slim, since only six articles had appeared in Oregon by then, much less in other states.

And Finally, a National Park

After seventeen years of vigorous action and perseverance, William Gladstone Steel's efforts paid off. During heated congressional debates over the bill to make Crater Lake a national park, Oregon Representative Thomas H. Tongue quoted renowned naturalist Professor Hart Merriam:

"Crater Lake is one of the most interesting natural objects on the continent, if not in the world. . . . Along the sides of the mountains there seem to be an unusual variety of fauna and flora, a great variety of timber, of mammal, birds, etc., rendering this place of great scientific value."

On April 21, 1902, the legislation was sent to the Senate, where it was assigned to the Committee on Public Lands. The Senate passed the bill without debate or amendment on May 9, 1902. President Theodore Roosevelt signed the bill on May 22nd, and Crater Lake became the seventh national park in the United States. When he heard about the signing, Steel wrote a letter to President Roosevelt expressing his thanks for the chief executive's active support in making his dream become a reality. Now the world would know what a spectacular place this was and it would be protected for all time. And it worked; celebrities began to arrive even though the landmark was still difficult to reach.

Famous author and outdoorsman Jack London visited the lake in 1911 with his wife Charmian Kittredge London and their Japanese cook, Nakata. London had never driven a team of horses before, but decided to make the 400-mile (643 km) trip by wagon from his Beauty Ranch in Glen Ellen, northern California, to Crater Lake in order to enjoy the scenery slowly. Arriving in Medford on August 11, London told reporters, "My wife and I are simply enjoying our mid-life honeymoon." The next day they accepted an automobile ride to Crater Lake. When interviewed by a local reporter after the trip, London said, "Of all the places we have visited, Crater Lake stands out as the most distinctive and impressive. Crater Lake is something to think about, not to talk or write about."

The Phantom Ship viewpoint offers a distant look at Wizard Island across the lake.

TOP: *This panoramic view of the island made William Gladstone Steel think of a wizard's hat.*

Unique Landscapes

The lake itself—its color, clarity, and reflective calmness—is not the only wondrous aspect of the Mount Mazama area. Another world exists deep below the lake, and the rock formations, plants, and animals inside the caldera and around the outside of the rim create a special environment to complement the beautiful lake.

Meanwhile, at the Bottom of the Lake

As I slowly sank into the depths of the lake, I was engulfed in blue which eventually turned to darkness. . . . After reaching the bottom on my dive to the deepest part of Crater Lake, I shut off the scrubbers and instrument lights to better experience the solitude and quiet, and to briefly reflect on being the first person to visit the deepest part of the lake.

—MARK BUKTENICA, Aquatic Biologist, 1988

From 1987 to 1989, scientists explored the bottom of Crater Lake with a one-person submarine, *Deep Rover*. This six-foot sphere of five-inch-thick acrylic plastic was equipped with large robotic arms to collect samples, making it look like a space-age crab. The sub was flown in by helicopter, and great care was taken to make no permanent impact on the environs during the research project.

Deep in the lake, in areas where hydrothermal fluids (warm mineral-rich water associated with volcanism) enter from under the lake bottom, scientists discovered large colonies of bacteria. These matted, interwoven yellow-orange organic masses hang from vertical rock spires or drape over lake floor outcroppings. Since they live in total darkness, these unusual organisms "feed" on geothermal heat instead of photosynthesis, which requires light.

Submarine pilot/researcher Mark Buktenica found stream-like channels two to three inches wide and deep coming from boulders around the Palisades on the northeast side of the lake. He found brilliant gold bacteria and blue mineral-rich pools where these channels ended at the lake bottom. In the deep waters below Skell Head, thirty-foot spires were formed by chemically rich hydrothermal fluids coming in contact with surrounding cold water, causing minerals to separate from the liquid and form solid chimneys around the geothermal liquids emerging from vents on the lake bottom. As a result of three years of field studies, scientists estimate that roughly two billion gallons of thermally and chemically enriched fluids flow into the bottom of Crater Lake every year.

Also, a thick band of moss circles the lake walls at depths of 85 to 460 feet below the surface. According to Mark Buktenica, "It hung like icicles on vertical cliffs and formed thick lush fields on the gentler slopes

The boat tour to Wizard Island allows visitors to see views of the lake unavailable from the rim, including this spring fed waterfall underneath Garfield Peak.

OPPOSITE: *The aptly named Phantom Ship sailing off for another adventure.*

around Wizard Island. The remarkable lower depth limit of 460 feet of these was due to the ability of light to penetrate deep into Crater Lake's clear water."

This exploration might have quelled the age-old rumors of the Crater Lake Monster. In 1884, the *Southwest Oregon Recorder* noted: "Crater Lake, Oregon, is inhabited by a dreadful monster. It is said to be as large as a man's body, two or three feet out of the water, and going at a rapid rate, as fast as a man could row a skiff, leaving a similar wave behind it." This sounds like a perfect description of the upright log, the Old Man of the Lake. This is not to be confused, however, with the 1977 horror film *The Crater Lake Monster*. The star of that movie is a giant plesiosaur, similar to the Loch Ness Monster. That one terrorizes a different Crater Lake in northern California. If submariner Buktenica saw anything of a monster down there, he is not talking about it. Or perhaps the monster has underwater hideouts. There are also tales of Bigfoot, also known as Sasquatch, in Crater Lake National Park, but there is no credible evidence for these stories.

Wizard Island

Wizard Island is a volcano inside a volcano at the west end of Crater Lake. It is a cinder cone volcano that rises about 763 feet (233 m) above the surface of the lake. At the top of the cone, there is a crater 300 feet (90 m) across and 90 feet (27 m) deep.

Over the next three or four hundred years after Mount Mazama's main eruption, smaller eruptions sealed the caldera floor with hardened lava. Then rain and snowmelt began to fill it up. While the water accumulated, smaller eruptions formed cinder cones on the lake bottom, but Wizard Island is the only one that rose above the water line. The erupting magma cooled quickly as it hit the air, solidifying into cinders that formed the cone. A second volcano, Merriam Cone, erupted completely underwater, forming what is known as "pillow lava." Scientists

Store: 270
576 Munson Valley Dr
Crater Lake
(541) 594-2255   Oregon
Oper: 232204

------------- RECEIPT -------------
                                    Trans #: 9760
                                    Register

9781940322179

Qty   Unit Pr.   Price   T

CRATER LAKE & BEYOND
1.000   19.95   19.95

                              Size: NOSZ

1.000 Piece(s)
                    Sub Total: 19.95
* Payments **
             Total ==>   19.95
             Payments ** =>   19.95

YPE
ACCOUNT TYPE   PURCHASE
CARD NUMBER   Mastercard
DATE/TIME   ***** **** *0373
REC #   06/12/18 18:29
INV/Chk #   00190
REFERENCE #   2612
SEQUENCE #   MK1193
UTH. #   943
TRY METHOD   0221
                      CHIP

XanterraCrater_Mi9
Xanterra Crater Lake Na, White City, OR
97503
541-830-0500

             $19.95

THANK YOU

C
           Issue
           MasterCard
           A0000000041010
           8000008000
           6800

is copy for yo

E
TOTAL
APPROVED
SETRAN/AAR...

MODE
APP
AID
TVR
TSI
ARC

PORTANT -- retain
rds.

MER COPY

6/1 ; 6:30 P

Wizard Island stands vigil while a summer thunderstorm brings a faint rainbow to the north rim.

OPPOSITE: *The trail to the summit of Wizard Island gives visitors an up-close look at the Witch's Cauldron—a caldera within the caldera.*

have one explanation for how Wizard Island was formed but the indigenous people have another.

According to Klamath Indian legend, the lords of the Above World (Skell) and the Below World (Llao) battled long ago. Mount Mazama crumbled in on itself and Crater Lake was born. In one version of the story, Skell chopped off Llao's head and flung it into the lake, forming an island. In 1885, Will Steel named the island "Wizard" "because of its weird appearance," shaped like a sorcerer's hat. He called the crater at the top of Wizard Island "Witches Cauldron" to complete the theme, although no one has ever heard of witches or wizards with an iron pot on top of their hat.

If you take the boat to Wizard Island, there is a rocky shore trail that takes you to Fumarole Bay on the southwest end of the island. The water along the shore is shallow, very clear, and often a scintillating emerald green. Its accessibility makes the bay a favorite spot for fishing and swimming.

TOP AND BOTTOM: *Like the "Horse of a Different Color" from* The Wizard of Oz, *the waters in Fumarole Bay can take on different hues—from blue to green to turquoise to clear—depending on your vantage point.*

Phantom Ship

The second-most interesting island, Phantom Ship, has craggy rock spires that make it look like a ship, and especially in dim light or fog it seems to disappear and then come back, like a ghost. Most of it is andesite, a variety of igneous rock, cooled magma that came to the surface underwater as much as 400,000 years ago. Geologists believe that it is a remnant of the first volcano to erupt in that area, long before Mount Mazama, making this the oldest exposed rock in the lake.

The ship sits on the southeast end of Crater Lake, rising 175 feet (200 m) above the surface. That's about as tall as a sixteen-story building. It is five hundred feet long, two hundred feet wide, and sits just below Dutton Cliff. Seven species of trees grow there, including sugar pine and lodgepole pine. Flocks of violet-green swallows live aboard the ship too, as well as several varieties of lichens and wildflowers.

Phantom Ship becomes even more mystical when it is silhouetted by the sunset.

BOTTOM: *A lake's-eye-view of Phantom Ship reveals that it is covered with several species of trees.*

Llao Rock

This female house finch calls Wizard Island home.

OPPOSITE: *One of the best places to see Crater Lake's other island is from the Phantom Ship Overlook on East Rim Drive.*

RIGHT: *Llao Rock, Crater Lake's most imposing rock face, rises nearly 2,000 feet above the lakeshore.*

Llao Rock is a massive gray cliff that formed when a lava flow filled an explosion crater on the north slope of the mountain before the big explosion that created the lake. It is named after Llao, the Klamath Indian god of the underworld. As mentioned earlier, his battles with Skell, the sky god, resulted in Mount Mazama's eruption and Crater Lake's creation. Llao Rock is the thickest lava layer found in the walls around Crater Lake. It is made of dacite, which is similar to andesite but it contains free quartz. At some points it is 1,200 feet thick. During the large Mazama eruption, part of that previous lava flow broke off and tumbled into the new caldera that formed after Mount Mazama collapsed. But the rest remained and jutted out from the inner rim as we see it today. It looms an imposing 1,800 feet (548 m) above the lake. One of the best ways to get an impressive first view of the lake is to start with the 1.5- to 2-mile round-trip hike that starts at the North Junction of Rim Drive. You climb 900 feet over an open pumice grade, and all of a sudden, there it is below you. At 8,049 feet (2,453 m) Llao Rock is the highest point on the northwest side of the lake.

On, In, or Around the Lake

There are dozens of geological wonders in Crater Lake itself, along its shores, and in the surrounding areas. Here are some of the most prominent.

Watchman Peak is a tremendous 2,000-foot-wide flow of andesite lava more than 400 feet thick. Its 8,013-foot height provides direct lake views to the east, the Rogue River Valley to the west, and the Klamath Basin to the south. William Gladstone Steel named the peak when he guided a survey in 1886. That year Steel and geologist Clarence Dutton mounted a United States Geological Survey study of the lake. With a small crew of men, they carried the *Cleetwood*, a half-ton survey boat, up the outside of Mount Mazama and then down into the caldera. With a piece of pipe fastened to a spool of piano wire, they measured the depth of 168 places on the bottom of the lake. On the same expedition, a professional topographer surveyed the area and made the first official map of the area. While measuring the depth of the lake, "a party of engineers was stationed on the summit to receive signals and record soundings."

Watchman Lookout Station No. 168 is one of two fire observation towers around the lake. Listed on the National Register of Historic Places in 1988, it serves as both a fire lookout and a museum. The current structure was erected in 1932.

Hillman Peak is a parasitic cone formed by one of Mount Mazama's volcanic side vents. At 8,156 feet, it is the highest point on the caldera's rim. When Mount Mazama collapsed, it cut the Hillman cone in half, revealing its insides. The spires on Hillman Peak are the cone's feeder tubes, which decomposed after conducting magma to the surface, taking on a yellow-orange hue from the gases and hot liquids they transported.

Although park founder William Gladstone Steel and others were quite creative in the naming of landforms around Crater Lake, none is as striking as "the Devil's Backbone." This spikey spine of dark rock just west of Wizard Island is the only volcanic dike in the caldera that snakes its way down from the rim a thousand feet down to the lakeshore. This 1,300-foot-long band of lava is about 50,000 years old.

Formations like this are formed when molten andesite forces its way up through cracks in the older layers of rock and then hardens. Then the

The Cleetwood, *a half-ton survey boat, was carried up Mount Mazama and then lowered down to the lakeshore for the Clarence Dutton expedition in 1886.*

Looking north from the Watchman fire lookout at dusk, with Rim Drive, Hillman Peak, and Llao Rock in the distance.

OPPOSITE: *The Devil's Backbone as seen from the North Junction viewpoint.*

outside rocks erode and decompose, leaving the vertical andesite plates standing like the spikes on the back of a dinosaur. The Backbone is fifty feet wide at the rim, but narrows to twenty-five feet near the lake. It rose up from deep inside a previous subterranean magma chamber that eventually gave rise to Mount Mazama.

To the east of Llao Rock you can see several more geological landmarks uniquely forged by volcanoes, weather, and time. On the north shore just opposite Mazama Village you can see Pumice Point, a big white dome-shaped clearing amid the trees and darker lava rock. This is a thick pile of dacite lump pumice. After the pumice was ejected from the chamber it was covered with a flow of andesite. Then glacial ice and its debris covered the two layers. Once the ice melted, new pumice explosions took place and covered the area with another 130- to 170-foot layer of pumice. Because very little grows in that area, you are looking at a formation that has not changed in thousands of years.

Farther east, the rim loses elevation as the north wall of the caldera blends into the east wall. At that point, the Palisades look like the wall of an old frontier log fort as a sheer wall of rock rises above the water near Cleetwood Cove. This is the only lava stream that flowed into the caldera during the big eruption instead of along the outside of the volcano. Less than six hundred feet above the lake, the Palisades are one massive lava flow, often covered with yellow lichen, making them a photogenic must-capture for visiting photographers.

The rugged geology of the Devil's Backbone comes into view from the surface of the lake.

BOTTOM: *Only a glimpse of the lichen-covered Palisades is visible from Rim Drive. It is best viewed from across the lake or from the boat tour.*

OPPOSITE TOP: *The Southwest meets the Middle Ages inside the Crater Lake caldera where the red rocks of Pumice Castle jut out of the mountainside like a fairy tale castle.*

OPPOSITE BOTTOM: *Although Phantom Ship is longer than a football field, it is dwarfed by Dutton Cliff.*

South of the Palisades is Pumice Castle, so named because of its shape and varied colors. Pumice Castle is a popular landmark along the caldera's east wall, and it is particularly photogenic just before sunset. Situated four hundred feet below the rim and 1,300 feet above the lake, the layers of brown, tan, pink, and brownish-red pumice are softer than most of the volcanic rock around it and so they erode faster, leaving a formation that reminds many people of a castle.

Looking over these formations to the southeast is Mount Scott. Known as a parasitic cone because it grew on the side of the larger Mount Mazama before its collapse, this 420,000-year-old stratovolcano's eastern slope shows the usual pyramid volcano shape, but its west side has been eroded by glaciers. Although the Klamath Indians call it Tum-sum-ne or Tomsandi, it is now named after Levi Scott, a nineteenth-century southern-Oregon explorer. At 8,926 feet (2,720 m), Mount Scott is the highest point in Crater Lake National Park.

Following the shore around to the south we find Dutton Cliff, probably the most distinctive landform along the rim except for Llao Rock. In addition to its steep face, the large u-shaped notches at either end of the cliff indicate where Sand and Sun Creeks cut through it. These canyons are yet another feature that were carved by icy glacial streams long before Mount Mazama collapsed.

The Pinnacles are needle-like rock formations projecting hundreds of feet high from the floor of Sand Canyon Creek. After Mount Mazama's big eruption but before its collapse, 200- to 300-foot-thick (60 to 90 m) beds of pumice and ash built up around the volcano. Over the years, steam and hot gases were released from the hot rocks underneath, flowing up to the surface through these pumice and ash beds. The extremely hot gas fused the ash and pumice it came in contact with into vents and tubes called fumaroles. Over thousands of years, erosion removed the surrounding pumice and left just the towering spires. The deep orange color at their base is caused when iron oxide or hematite interacts with water, leaching out rust stains just like exposed metal or on bathroom fixtures.

Closest to Rim Village, Garfield Peak is 7,976 feet, (2,431 m) tall. William Steel named the peak after President Theodore Roosevelt's Secretary of the Interior, James R. Garfield, who was also the third son of President James A. Garfield and an early visitor to Crater Lake.

Because of solfataric action (mineral transformation resulting from volcanic vents spewing sulfurous gases and steam), the rocks present shades of brown, buff, orange, and yellow instead of the typical andesite blacks and grays. Even though the 1.7-mile Garfield Peak Trail is rated difficult because the climb is about 900 feet, it is one of the most popular because of its nearness to Rim Village and one of the best bird's-eye views of the lake from the top of the trail.

TOP: *A bit off the beaten path, the Pinnacles are yet another fantastic volcanic formation.*

RIGHT: *The trail to Garfield Peak begins at the Crater Lake lodge and ends in another world.*

OPPOSITE TOP: *The lowest point of the rim above the water is Sun Notch.*

OPPOSITE BOTTOM: *In 1907, James R. Garfield, Secretary of the Interior under President Theodore Roosevelt and third son of President James A. Garfield, attended this lakeside picnic. He is fourth on the left.*

How Do We "Know" That Crater Lake Is Blue?

For more than a century, people have been raving about Crater Lake's beautiful deep blue color. But how do we know it *is* blue? Philosophers and scientists describe objects as having properties or qualities. Some, like size, shape, hot, cold, wet, and dry exist within the object itself. Color, however, depends on the observer. The human brain and eyes cooperate to translate light into what we call color. Merriam-Webster's dictionary defines color as: "a phenomenon of light (as red, brown, pink, or blue) or visual perception that enables one to differentiate otherwise identical objects."

Since language developed, we have agreed that apples are red, bananas are yellow, and the sky is blue. We don't even know if we all see those colors the same way, and people who are color-blind definitely do not see the same thing that average people do.

Water looks blue because its molecules absorb sunlight in specific ways. When light hits a surface, it is reflected, scattered, or absorbed. If objects scatter all wavelengths of light, they appear white. If they absorb all wavelengths, they appear black. Water molecules scatter the light, and the blue color reflects back to our eyes. Larger bodies of water absorb long-wavelength colors, such as red, orange, and yellow, and also at the short-wave end of the spectrum, removing violet and ultraviolet. That leaves blue wavelengths remaining visible to most human eyes.

The amount of blue depends on how much water is together in one place. The deeper the water is, the more it can absorb the other colors, and the bluer it appears. A glass of water does not look blue because it doesn't contain enough molecules to absorb the light, but a swimming pool does look blue, unless it gets too dirty.

If there are impurities, sediment, algae, or things floating on the water it may look green, reddish brown, or a combination of several hues. At Crater Lake, the blueness is most intense where extraneous particles and algae are low. Since muddy streams do not feed Crater Lake, and it is extremely deep, it has a beautiful sapphire blue color, especially in bright sunlight.

An American kestrel peeps out from a nesting box.

BELOW: *Historic Crater Lake Lodge under a fresh blanket of snow.*

The Villages, Natural and Unobtrusive

Since the formation of the National Park Service in 1916, and even before that, the general plan has been to make staff and visitor buildings blend into the landscape in order to let the natural beauty of the area stand out. The architects and designers have been quite successful in carrying out their vision all across the United States, and the buildings in Crater Lake National Park are good examples of their work.

Shortly after Crater Lake became a national park, Steel raised the idea to build a lodge to accommodate visitors. In 1909, he convinced Portland contractor Alfred Parkhurst to build it. In July 1907, the newly incorporated Crater Lake Company set up "Camp Crater" on the rim, providing meals and sleeping areas for up to fifty visitors at a time. Steel organized boat tours and talked of plans for more hotels and even installing an elevator from the rim to the shore. When Parkhurst became manager in 1909, he added oil stoves for heating and wooden floors in the tents.

Construction began on the stone foundation and wooden-framed lodge that same year. Designing for such a heavy-snow area was a challenge. It was expensive to haul building materials over unpaved mountain roads, and the work could only be done three months of the year. The job got done, but Parkhurst cut costs by covering the building with tar paper, using cardboard for inside walls, and not including toilets in the guest rooms.

Nevertheless, visitors flocked to the lodge when it opened in 1915, because it was better than camping in tents. A 1922 upgrade doubled the number of rooms, and some now had private baths. Registration dropped drastically during the Great Depression, but the second- and third-floor rooms were completed in the mid-1930s despite financial hard times.

Crater Lake Lodge was closed to the public during World War II, but increased tourism after the war benefitted the lodge. Management still had a great deal of trouble maintaining the lodge in such a remote area with extreme weather conditions, especially since its peak season only lasted three or four months.

The National Park Service purchased the lodge in 1967, but funding for maintenance was still difficult and deterioration continued. There were plans to demolish the building, but public opposition saved the old lodge. The building closed in 1989, and after two years of planning, reconstruction began in 1991.

Finally, between 1991 and 1995, Crater Lake Lodge was completely rebuilt. The building was completely rearranged on the inside, although the outside appears the same. There are now 71 rooms instead of 101. Each room has a nice new retro, black-and-white tile bathroom. The foundation and exterior shingles were replaced. Since all the renovations and replacements retained the original type of materials, shapes, and colors, it is still listed on the National Registry of Historic Places. They did such a great job that it is hard to remember that you are not staying in a 1920s-style great lodge.

About a third of a mile west of the lodge along a nice walkway with a view down to the lake lies the Rim Village Café. This cafeteria-style café is quick and easy, and the second floor has great views of the lake. In between the lodge and café are the Rim Village Visitor Center and the Sinnott Memorial Overlook. You will also find the Crater Lake Trolley parked along the sidewalk across from the visitor center. Park rangers join each two-hour bus tour to provide detailed information on the geology, wildlife, and history of the park.

If you want to get the full experience of the lake, a cruise is one of the best ways to do it. You can take a standard cruise around the lake, or spend time hiking and exploring Wizard Island via the shuttle. There is

Pine siskins inhabit vine maples at lower elevations.

The trolley parked at Rim Village after a long day of showing tourists the majesty of Crater Lake.

Although Crater Lake Lodge closes for the winter, the Rim Village Café is open year-round.

one warning, though. The caldera walls rise up steeply around the lake, the route from the rim to the Cleetwood Cove landing is more than a mile, and you walk down 700 feet (213 m) along the way. For many, the hike back up at a steep 11% grade is even more difficult. Because of this trail, the tour is not recommended for people with physical problems, especially ailments aggravated at higher elevations.

Like the trolley, the boat tours feature a park ranger who provides information and points out the various landmarks as the boat travels around the lake. The views aboard the boat are outstanding, especially the water's clarity and various colors. You can also take the boat to Wizard Island, stay three hours exploring, picnicking, fishing, or swimming, and then catch the shuttle back to the mainland.

The Steel Visitor Center and Gift Shop is three miles south of Rim Village in the park headquarters area at the southern entrance to the park. There is a U.S. post office in the same building, and the park's administration building, completed in 1936, is right next to it.

If you take the short trail behind the Steel Visitor Center, you will run across a three-foot-high sculpture chiseled out of volcanic rock. Earl Russell Bush, a 31-year-old medical doctor who took care of the Crater Lake road crew, used his spare time to try some creative rock carving. He designed his first work in the realistic, muscular style of Auguste Rodin, the father of modern sculpture. By the end of the summer work season in September 1917, Dr. Bush had less injuries to care for and he could spend more time on the sculpture. By the time he left in late October his artwork was complete. He preferred to leave it unmarked, but photographer Fred Kiser named it Lady of the Woods in 1930 and marked it with a sign. Like many features at Crater Lake National Park, the sculpture gives the place an old-fashioned personal touch and you can imagine tourists from half a century ago looking at the same objects you are viewing today.

Seven miles farther south on the park road is another hunting-lodge-style set of buildings: Mazama Village at the Annie Spring entrance to Crater Lake National Park. Here you will find the Mazama Campground, one of two campgrounds available in the park, and "The Cabins at Mazama," advertised as "no frills lodging in a pine forest." The Annie Creek Restaurant and Gift Shop is a good mid-point choice between fine dining at the Crater Lake Lodge and the snack bar style of the Rim Village Café. This family-style restaurant serves breakfast, lunch, and dinner, including pizza and a soup and salad bar.

Crater Lake Flora and Fauna

The lake's geography, geology, and climate provide a unique habitat for a wide variety of plants and animals. Trees on the mountain include mountain hemlock, lodgepole pine, whitebark pine, Shasta red fir, sugar pine, and ponderosa pine, and many of them are in old-growth forests where some have survived more than five centuries.

According to the National Park Service, an "old-growth forest" is one in which growth has been undisturbed for at least 250 years. At nearby Mount Rainier, some stands of trees may be 1,000 years old. Here in Crater Lake National Park, you will find examples of trees that are not found in commercial logging tree plantations. Aging trees with defects, dead trees, and fallen logs in old-growth forests are important to creating a varied habitat. Here, standing dead trees (called snags) and dead logs are allowed to remain in place, providing homes for bugs, birds, and chipmunks, and the dead trees provide fertilizer as they decompose.

At Crater Lake National Park's highest elevations, you will find the whitebark pine. They can survive in extremely severe conditions, but are often small, twisted, and gnarled, looking more like shrubs than trees. Near Cloudcap on the East Rim Drive, you can see a good stand of these hardy survivors.

This gnarled goddess greets tourists across the road from the Watchman Peak trailhead on Rim Drive.

BELOW: *A Clark's nutcracker flies into a dead tree above Wizard Island on a moody day.*

OPPOSITE ABOVE: *The Godfrey Glen Trail near the south entrance offers visitors a short hike to an amazing overlook of Munson Canyon.*

OPPOSITE BELOW: *Union Creek flows into the Rogue River a few miles south of the national park.*

Old Man of the Lake

For more than a century, "the Old Man of the Lake" has been bobbing around vertically in the ice-cold lake water. No one is concerned, though, because he's a full-sized tree, not a person. The old man floats leisurely, blown about by the wind in patterns that resemble a billiard ball carom, zigzagging from one shore to another. No one seems to know how long this "tree-sicle" will survive, since the low water temperature slows the bobbing tree's decomposition.

Crater Lake's Late Bloomers

The elevation at the base of Mount Mazama is 4,000 feet, and the highest point is more than 8,000 feet. There are snowdrifts on the mountain in late May, and the snow doesn't melt until July (although there are patches in shady areas even in late August). Like the Never Summer Mountains at the source of the Colorado River, late spring blends into early fall with no official summer season in between. Similarly, Anchorage, Alaska, residents claim that they do indeed have a summer—"We call it the Fourth of July."

According to Elmer Applegate in his 1937 *Nature Notes* article, "The Flowering Seasons of Crater Lake Plants," there are more than five hundred sixty flowering plant species that grow in the park, but only a quar-

The Old Man of the Lake drifts into a cove at water's edge.

BELOW: *Springtime in September: At around 7,000 feet in elevation, many of the Rim's wildflowers don't bloom until late summer.*

44

Lewis's monkey flower.

TOP: *When the Castle Crest Wildflower Gardens are in full bloom, it looks more like Hawaii than Oregon.*

ter of these could be considered wildflowers. The most common varieties are Indian paintbrush, lupine, monkey flower, Pasque flower, penstamen, and shooting star.

In "Wandering Through Wildflowers," *Nature Notes* volume 27, 1996, Oregon State University Professor Peter Zika reports that some of the first flowers to appear in late spring are western flowering dogwood, Shelton's violet, and pink fairy slippers. Elsewhere, "legions of lupines and scarlet paintbrushes greet you when summer's heat has opened the footpaths along Annie Creek and into the Castle Crest Wildflower Garden."

As snowfields melt on Garfield Park Trail east of Crater Lake Lodge, Zika says you may enjoy "the blue blossoms of squaw carpet," or later in the summer the brilliant pink and purple penstamens. Pink and yellow monkey flowers bloom in midsummer, and the brilliant yellow rabbit-brush blooms late in the year because its deep root system can access stored water.

The Castle Crest Wildflower Garden is one of the first pullouts on the East Rim Drive, not far from the park headquarters. The half-mile trail from the parking area circles around meadows often bursting with wildflowers in the spring.

In addition to wildflowers, there are several fruit-bearing shrubs in the area. The Crater Lake currant can be found in many parts of southwestern Oregon, but the majority of plants are found in Crater Lake National Park. The currant is a trailing shrub with red berries and copper-colored flowers that is found in the subalpine elevations among the mountain hemlocks. Three miles east of the gardens on the Rim Drive you will find Vidae Falls, one of the prettiest waterfalls close to Crater Lake.

Currant berries add a dash of color to a downed tree on the Lady of the Woods Trail behind Steel Visitor Center.

OPPOSITE: *Vidae Falls is not only beautiful but also one of the most accessible features in the park, visible from a pullout on East Rim Drive.*

RIGHT: *William G. Steel looks on as kitchen workers feed the bears, an activity definitely forbidden now.*

Afoot, Under the Waves, and on the Wing

NATIONAL PARK SERVICE

Bears, bobcats, and pine martins are rarely seen around Crater Lake, but they are there nonetheless. You may see deer and marmots (they seem to be used to people), and golden mantle ground squirrels are often seen near the trails and overlooks.

In July 1928, the first issue of *Nature Notes* was published by the Crater Lake National Park staff. We are grateful to the Crater Lake Institute for making these informative and often delightful volumes available online. Here is an excerpt from "Our Bears," by Earl U. Homuth, volume 2, number 1, July 1929: "A yearling cub became so intimate with the 'bug crew,' which has been working on pine bark beetle eradication, that several men have had to spend lunchless days in the forest. Lunches are now suspended from the ends of small branches. Another yearling has been developing the habit of begging or demanding food from tourists entering on the Medford road. He is reported by those coming in on this road nearly every day."

Of course today's tourists have to be reminded constantly "Do NOT feed the animals in the park!" The bears have become scarce now that there are plenty

A marmot makes a brief appearance and then disappears back into its hole.

more tourists around, but birds, not limited to the ground and able to get away from humans quickly, thrive in Crater Lake National Park. Because of their ability to travel easily over difficult terrain and find food even in burned-out areas, birds are found in every region of the park. Among the most common are Clark's nutcracker, jays, red-tailed hawks, spotted owls, mountain bluebirds, and even bald eagles.

There are no native fish in the lake, but humans introduced several species from 1888 until 1941. Visitors are encouraged to catch as many of the two remaining species, rainbow trout and Kokanee salmon as they want. No license is necessary, but fishermen must use lures or tied flies so that organic bait does not pollute the lake. All fish must be removed from the lake. You can catch all you want, but no throwing any back in.

There's More Than a Beautiful Blue Lake

The lake may be the star of the show, but there are many fascinating things to see inside and within a few miles of Crater Lake National Park, including but not limited to mountain peaks, waterfalls, crystal clear creeks, and even a desert made of pumice.

The Pumice Desert is a broad flat in the northern section of the park three miles north of the lake on West Rim Drive. This desert was covered with pumice and ash more than 200 feet deep in some places by the explosion of Mount Mazama. Soil-enriching organic matter is scarce in

Although river otters don't inhabit the lake itself, they can be found on nearly the entire length of the Rogue River, which begins within the borders of the park.

BOTTOM: *A Clark's nutcracker scuttles about on a mountain hemlock.*

OPPOSITE RIGHT: *A short drive from thickly wooded forests and rushing waterfalls, the Pumice Desert seems like it's from a different world.*

OPPOSITE BOTTOM: *A curious barred owl peers down from the branch of a pine tree.*

the Pumice Desert, making it difficult for anything to grow. After thousands of years, scattered groups of lodgepole pines have just started intruding along the edges of the desert.

Natural Wonders to the North of the Lake

Past the Pumice Desert you will see Mount Thielsen's craggy point in front of you as you leave the north entrance of the park. Since volcanic activity stopped there about 250,000 years ago, glaciers have drastically eroded Thielsen's usual pyramid structure and created steep jagged slopes similar to the Matterhorn in the Alps. Because of its distance from other peaks and its height, 9,184 feet (2,799 m), this former volcano is known as "The Lightning Rod." The numerous lightning strikes create unusual mineral formations called fulgurites, sometimes called petrified lightning. When extremely hot lightning melts silica or other electricity-conducting minerals and fuses them into a mass, it produces hollow glassy tubes from two to five inches long and about a quarter inch in diameter, covered with glassy crystal knobs.

No hike down the rim to Cleetwood Cove would be complete without one of Crater Lake's resident golden-mantled ground squirrels scurrying about at your feet.

OPPOSITE: *Viewable from several points along the rim, Mount Thielsen is the most ubiquitous Crater Lake landmark that isn't actually in the park.*

TOP: *A closer view of Mount Thielsen from nearby Lemolo Lake.*

Even though Crater Lake is almost a lava-sealed basin and not the source of any river or creek, any area with that much precipitation and high mountains is bound to produce some outstanding rivers that attract sportsmen from around the world for the fishing, rafting, and kayaking adventures.

The Umpqua, North Umpqua, and South Umpqua are three prominent rivers whose tributaries begin with water rivulets of melting glaciers and snow not far from Crater Lake. The South Umpqua River begins about twenty miles northwest of Crater Lake. It travels through part of the Cascade Range for 115 miles (185 km) before it joins the North Umpqua.

From its source just north of Mount Thielsen, the North Umpqua River flows north and west 106 miles (171 km) and joins the South Umpqua. The scenic North Umpqua, known for its emerald-green waters, drains the Cascade Range southeast of Eugene, Oregon, flowing through steep rugged canyons surrounded by large forests of Douglas firs. The North Umpqua is one of the best fly-fishing streams in the Pacific Northwest, or maybe even the world, according to some avid anglers.

The two rivers meet near Roseburg, Oregon, to form the Umpqua River, one of the major rivers of the Oregon Coast. It is 111 miles long (179 km) and is known for its bass and shad fishing. The Umpqua drains

The trail to Fall Creek Falls along the North Umpqua River reveals a much more lush world than exists higher up at Crater Lake.

numerous valleys west of the Cascades and south of the Willamette Valley. It flows north and west through the Oregon Coast Range and drains into the Pacific Ocean at Winchester Bay.

About forty-seven miles north of Crater Lake on Oregon Highway 138 lies one of the best-known falls in southern Oregon. Here, the North Umpqua River carved a jagged gorge to create the 113-foot Toketee Falls. The name means "pretty" or "graceful" in the Chinook language. The upper section plunges 40 feet into a pool settled in a deep alcove. Then the water plunges another 85 feet over a sheer wall of volcanic basalt into a larger pool. The water is then diverted into a 12-foot-diameter wooden pipeline to an electrical generator downstream. This control element helps regulate the flow so that the waterfall is fairly consistent throughout the year.

South-central Oregon is a naturalist's dream, ranging from volcanoes to deserts to rushing waterfalls in primeval forests and back again, all within a one-hundred-mile radius. Eighty miles northeast of the Pumice Desert in the Deschutes National Forest just south of Bend, Oregon, lies Newberry National Volcanic Monument. This 54,000-acre (2,898 ha) parcel in the Lava Lands of central Oregon includes lakes, lava flows, and remarkable geologic features. At 7,985 feet (2,434 m) Paulina Peak is the highest point in the monument. Newberry Crater, another name for the area, refers to a seventeen-square-mile caldera formed when a volcano the size of the state of Rhode Island erupted and collapsed. This caldera is still seismically and geothermally active and sits on a pool of magma thousands of feet deep. There are more than four hundred vents and cinder cones in the area, as well as solidified rivers of rhyolite obsidian, which looks like big chunks of smoky volcanic glass.

Another highlight of the Umpqua National Forest is Watson Falls.

OPPOSITE: *Arguably the prettiest waterfall in southern Oregon, Toketee Falls carves its way through a cliff of columnar basalt.*

One of the main attractions at the monument is the Big Obsidian Flow, the only one like it on Earth. They call the area "Big Obsidian," and its formation occurred in three stages. First a gas-rich explosion produced a high column of tephra (rocks and ash). Pumice covered the southern part of the caldera and wind blew it to the east flank of the volcano. Strong winds carried some of the tephra several hundred miles east into Idaho. Then a not-as-explosive second eruption produced the Paulina Lake flow of ash between the Big Obsidian Flow and the lake. During the last stage of this eruption, magma with very little gas flowed over the surface and formed a dome where the vent was. Then came the Big Obsidian Flow, natural glass that cools quickly with very little crystal growth.

Paulina Falls is the first of many gorgeous destinations in Newberry Volcanic National Monument.

TOP: *A mountaintop you can drive to: Paulina Peak overlooks the Big Obsidian Flow and East Lake.*

Marvels West of the Lake

The Rogue River is the biggest and most famous of southwest Oregon's three major rivers. Before the great explosion when Mount Mazama was still 12,000 feet tall, the Rogue began at what is now called Boundary Springs. As the mountain collapsed, a glowing hot pumice avalanche thundered forty miles downstream in just a few minutes, covering the spring. But the water found its way, carving a hundred-foot canyon in the volcanic debris, and then tumbling over a 15-foot waterfall.

The river flows about 215 miles (346 km) and is known for its salmon runs and whitewater rafting. Its descent takes it back through time from the geologically younger High Cascades, down through the older Western Cascades, and through the more ancient Klamath Mountains. There, in the Kalmiopsis Wilderness area near the Pacific Coast, the river flows over some of the best examples of rocks from the earth's mantle.

Archaeological excavations of the terrace at Stratton Creek just off the Rogue River and forty-two miles east of the coast show that the land hosted human occupants beginning in the Early Holocene, 12,000 years ago. They made stone tools and ground pigments for paints, and the materials found there show that they engaged in long-range trading into northern California.

A bullfrog basks in a pond near the banks of the Rogue River.

TOP: *The Rogue River begins its journey to the sea at Boundary Springs in the northwestern corner of Crater Lake National Park.*

Archaeologists say that several thousand years later, after Mount Mazama's eruption, activity in the area intensified, probably as more people arrived from other places. Researchers found more obsidian tools, more prevalent in volcanic areas like what is now Lava Beds National Monument. They focused more on salmon and shellfish and began to cook their food in stone-lined pits.

European fur trappers entered the area, followed by prospectors motivated by the California Gold Rush. Cultural clashes resulted in the Rogue River Wars, 1855–56. After dozens of deaths of Indians, settlers, and soldiers, the Natives were removed to reservations outside the Rogue River basin. Settlers then moved in to the remote lower basin, which now has one of only two remaining rural mail-boat routes in the United States. Populations on the Rogue River west of Medford are still sparse, but there are many hiking trails, public parks, and campgrounds.

Cormorants hoot and holler at Hyatt Lake in the Cascade-Siskiyou National Monument, which straddles the Oregon/California border south of Crater Lake.

Rogue Gorge, located just upriver from Union Creek Resort, is accessible via a pullout on Crater Lake Highway.

TOP RIGHT: *Madrone trees overlook Barr Creek Falls, which cascades 175 feet into the Rogue River.*

Famous Fishermen

*Pure as the snow from which it sprang, the river
had its source in the mountain under Crater Lake.*
—ZANE GREY, *Rogue River Feud*, 1925

In 1919, one of the American West's first and all-time bestselling authors, Zane Grey, first visited Oregon to fish Crater Lake and the Rogue River. He came back to the Rogue several times in the 1920s, and a chapter in his book *Tales of Fresh Water Fishing* is about his 1925 driftboat trip on the lower Rogue. His 1929 novel, *Rogue River Feud*, centers on a villainous salmon-packing tycoon. Grey switched streams in the 1930s, preferring the North Umpqua to the Rogue. Zane Grey's books made fly-fishing for salmon and steelhead popular and gave the Umpqua and Rogue their international reputations as renowned trout and steelhead dream streams. Grey's cabin at Winkle Bar on the remote lower Rogue River is now owned and preserved by the Bureau of Land Management and is open to the public.

In the 1930s, Hollywood stars and even top politicians were "gone fishin'" on the Rogue River. At a star-studded Los Angeles diner, Clark

A mountain ash tree clings to the rocks on the banks of the Upper Rogue.

OPPOSITE TOP: *A footpath along the Upper Rogue in Prospect takes you to Mill Creek Bridge, which dates back to 1923.*

OPPOSITE BOTTOM: *Three of the Upper Rogue's most striking features: moss, lichen, and mist.*

Gable was overheard saying "Well, I'd rather be eating flapjacks at the Weasku Inn" (on the Rogue River east of Grants Pass). Ginger Rogers loved the Rogue River, and President Herbert Hoover fished there too.

After accepting the Republican Party nomination for President of the United States, Herbert Hoover drove from his home in Palo Alto, California, up through Oregon's Coastal Range on a whirlwind fishing trip with eleven photographers, sixteen reporters, and his son Allan, plus a few dozen others following along. He had fished the Rogue River several times before, and claimed it was "the best fishing in the West."

Hoover liked Bill Isaac's Big Rock Lodge. The owner of a men's clothing store in Medford, Isaac had spread the word far and wide about the steelhead fishing in the area. On this pre-election trip, clad in waist-high waders, Hoover stepped into the river at 5 a.m. on July 30th, looking for just the right fishing spot. Harassed by loud photographers splashing around trying to get a close up, Hoover caught no fish that day. According to Bill Miller in the *Oregon Mail Tribune*, Hoover was quite irritated and said, "The most sacred time next to prayer, is when a man tries to fish."

Although they love the remote wilderness, even outdoorsmen have to come into town once in a while for supplies. On the Rogue River, Medford is the major place to go for that.

Medford in the Middle

Just eight miles south of the Rogue River on Interstate 5, and eighty miles southwest of Crater Lake, Medford, Oregon, is the fourth largest populated area in the state, with a metropolitan-area population of 208,545 in 2014. Surveyors for the Oregon and California Railroad reached the area in 1883, making it a relative latecomer as far as settlements go. Nearby Jacksonville was considered, but the engineers opted for a spot at the middle ford of Bear Creek in November 1883. Railroad engineer David Loring named the town after Medford, Massachusetts, near his hometown of Concord. The Massachusetts Medford was also a "middle ford," and the word comes from "med," which is a Latin prefix for "middle," and "ford," meaning a place to cross a river.

Like similar towns near major rivers and wilderness areas, Medford is a hub for sportsmen. There are more than a dozen sporting goods stores, and almost as many whitewater rafting tour companies. Situated in a river valley, Medford's elevation is 1,382 feet (421 m) above sea level. Surrounded by mountains, temperatures are relatively mild in all four seasons with an average rainfall of 18 to 20 inches and annual snowfall of three to four inches. The climate is almost perfect for farming, ranching, and just plain living. Halfway between San Francisco and Portland, Medford claims the honor and responsibility of being the financial, medical, and tourist hub of southern Oregon.

From East Vilas Road in Medford, take a right on Crater Lake highway and you'll reach the national park in about an hour and a half.

OPPOSITE: *Mount McLoughlin reflects in Fourmile Lake in the appropriately named Sky Lakes Wilderness.*

One of the Rogue Valley's numerous pear orchards in bloom beneath the sheer cliffs of Lower Table Rock.

Table Rocks

A popular destination for hikers and wildflower lovers, the wide-angle view from the top of the rocks is worth the trip. To the east you can see Mount McLoughlin as it tops the Cascade Range, and looking to the south and west from the top of Table Rocks you have a great view of the Siskiyou Mountains. Looking north from the same vantage point, the mountain forests of the Rogue-Umpqua Divide complete your 360-degree view.

Seven million years ago an andesite lava flow, followed by millions of years of erosion after the flow, formed two plateaus just north of the Rogue River near Medford, Oregon. Called Upper Table Rock and Lower Table Rock because of their position (not differing elevations), their flat tops rise dramatically 800 feet above the Rogue River Valley below.

Archaeologists have determined that prehistoric cultures lived here 15,000 years ago, making it one of Oregon's oldest inhabited sites. The rocks' unique structure made them gathering places for Native Americans, prospectors, and migrating settlers along the Applegate Trail.

Seventy species of animals and three hundred forty species of plants,

including two hundred wildflower species, live on the Table Rocks, taking advantage of the pools formed in impermeable andesite surfaces during the winter and spring rainy seasons. The mesa tops are covered with a mosaic of seasonal pools, stony flats, and grassy hills. These mesas come alive with wildflowers in the spring, truly a sight to behold.

And there are still more interesting things to see to the south and west. Backtracking again through Medford and on to the south, an older settlement grew up into one of Oregon's most unusual cities.

Ashland: A Park, a University, and a Festival

About sixteen miles north of the California-Oregon border, near Interstate 5, the city of Ashland is best known for its world-renowned Oregon Shakespeare Festival. Southern Oregon University began as the Ashland Academy in 1872 and after several closings and restarts settled at its current location in 1926.

The first known inhabitants along Ashland Creek were the Shasta people, who lived a semi-nomadic lifestyle in the forests and mountains along creeks that fed into the Shasta, Klamath, and Scott Rivers of north-central California and south-central Oregon. There were about 6,000 of them before Hudson's Bay Company fur trappers spread malaria there in the 1830s, and by 1851 there were only 3,000 natives left. By 1853, a gold mining boom at the Klamath-Trinity mines led to the tribe's violent decimation by Euro-American settlers, reducing the tribe to just 300 members.

An egret takes a drink from a pond in Ashland.

For much of the 20th century, the historic Ashland Springs Hotel was the tallest building between San Francisco and Portland.

LEFT: *Ashland is nestled in the foothills of the Siskiyou Mountains, the highest point of which is home to Mount Ashland Ski Area.*

OPPOSITE: *The crown jewel of Ashland is 100-acre Lithia Park, located just off the Plaza in downtown. This is the Torii Gate at the entrance of the Japanese Garden.*

Gold was discovered at Rich Gulch in 1851 and the tent city of Jacksonville formed along its banks about sixteen miles northwest of what would become Ashland. Abel Helman and Eber Emery constructed a flourmill near what is now the entrance to Lithia Park in 1852. Originally called Ashland Mill, it was named for Helman's home, Ashland County, Ohio.

Established in the early 1900s, one of the city's best features is Lithia Park, ninety-three acres of forested canyon lands stretching about fifteen miles along Ashland Creek from its headwaters near Mount Ashland all the way to the city's downtown plaza. The name comes from lithium oxide found in the stream water. The park has a band shell, an ice skating rink, and miles of hiking trails.

The Ashland Springs Hotel and the Allen Elizabethan Theater seen from the mountains above town.

The Bard Comes to Ashland

It started with the remains of an old Chautauqua building and a man of vision, Angus L. Bowmer. Although not connected with the Chautauqua movement, it is appropriate that Bowmer's Shakespeare program began there, since it too was a cultural adult education program. Named for the first meetings at Chautauqua Lake, New York, Chautauqua was part of a larger adult education movement that began in the early nineteenth century.

In early America, few adults got more than an eighth-grade education, especially in rural areas. To meet their thirst for knowledge, Josiah Holbrook founded the Lyceum in 1826. It was a series of debates, lectures, and discussions for adults on politics, philosophy, and culture, often held in tents. Lecturers and performers traveled from town to town on a "lyceum circuit." By the 1920s, hundreds of informal organizations offered more than 3,000 lyceum-type programs all over the United States. Chautauqua was the largest and most organized of these lyceum organizations. It was that tradition of bringing culture to rural areas that Bowmer carried on in Ashland.

Bowmer was born in Bellingham, Washington, in 1904, graduated from Washington State Normal School in 1923, and attended the University of Washington in Seattle in the 1930s and appeared in several Shakespeare plays there. He taught English at Southern Oregon Normal School in Ashland from 1931 to 1971.

In 1935, Bowmer persuaded Ashland's officials to revive traditional July 4th celebrations, but with a new twist, a Shakespearean festival. Bowmer, along with local citizens, students, and teachers, performed *Merchant of Venice* and *Twelfth Night.*

Beginning as a summer outdoor series, the festival now lasts from February to October, presenting a wide variety of plays at three theaters. The festival grew over seventy years, and has become an award-winning and internationally known regional theater company. The Oregon Shakespeare Festival is now the largest repertory theater in the United States.

In addition, the Oregon Cabaret Theater, opened in 1986, produces dinner theater musicals and comedy throughout the year.

From bards to bats, southern Oregon certainly has a wide variety of experiences. It's only thirty-six miles as the crow flies from Ashland to the Oregon Caves, but since we are not birds we are obliged to take a long and winding road—eighty-three miles and almost two hours—through the forested Siskiyou Mountains to one of the few arrays of marble caverns in the world.

A column, stalagmite, and stalactite in Oregon Caves.

Oregon Caves National Monument

Thousands of years ago, primeval forest rainwater seeped into underground marble formations and created the Oregon Caves in the Siskiyou Mountains of southwestern Oregon, affectionately known as "The Marble Halls." The National Park Service manages 3,900 caves in the United States, and only two others, Great Basin National Park and Kings Canyon National Park are marble caves. Oregon Caves National Monument is 480 acres (194 ha) set aside around an extensive system of underground marble chambers created by mineral-laden water penetrating deep into fractures in the rock formations. Dripping water formed fantastic stalactite and stalagmite formations.

The Takelma Indians lived in villages along the Rogue and Illinois River Valleys for thousands of years before the Anglo-Europeans arrived. They speared salmon and hunted deer and small game, and ate camas roots, acorns, and wild berries. It is estimated that 90% of the tribe died of smallpox epidemics in the 1780s, spread to them by other Natives before they ever encountered the explorers and fur trappers. Although Native Takelma Indians lived near the caves along the fertile Applegate and Rogue River Valleys, there is no evidence that they ever entered them.

Just like almost every other place in Oregon in the 1820s, Hudson Bay fur trappers explored and trapped for pelts in the area. As was often the case in American history, the trappers were followed by prospectors looking for gold in the 1830s. The safer Applegate Trail through southern Oregon brought more settlers, and the area's Anglo population began to grow.

Gold was found near Waldo in the Illinois Valley in 1851. The next five years brought violence between settlers, prospectors, and Natives. The Takelmas were forcibly relocated to the Siletz Reservation on the central Oregon Coast in 1856, joined by their neighbors, the Athapaskans and the Shasta. The gold was not as plentiful as expected, but settlers and miners remained and took up farming and hunting as the area responded to the large demand for timber as well.

A hunter named Elijah Davidson discovered the caves in 1874. The story has it that his hunting dog Bruno found the entrance and Davidson followed him in, even though he might have met a bear face-to-face while doing so.

The main part of the monument is twenty miles east of Cave Junction in the Siskiyou Mountains near the Rogue River. President William Howard Taft established Oregon Caves National Monument in 1909. The name "Oregon Caves" is misleading because the main attraction is a 15,000-foot (4,600 m) marble passage cave system, though eight separate smaller caves have also been discovered in the monument.

They are solutional caves, resulting from a process in which bacteria devour dead plants and animals and then emit carbon dioxide that makes the groundwater acidic. It then seeps through cracks in the rock and dissolves the bedrock over millions of years.

Sometimes this process works in reverse, and the minerals dissolved by the water harden again. When water with a lot of dissolved calcite drips from the roof of the cave onto the floor, some of the minerals are left behind as a precipitate. These residues grow and create flowstone and dripstone stalactites and stalagmites.

Cave crickets, also called camel crickets, can grow to up to eight inches long.

BELOW: *A gray fox searches for prey in an oak savanna.*

In some unusual cases, like this one at Oregon Caves, the original limestone minerals metamorphosed into marble through heat and pressure. This transfiguration from limestone to marble happened 160 million years ago at the same time the Klamath Mountains were formed, but the caves themselves are probably a mere two or three million years old. The water in the main cave comes from Upper Cave Creek, which is then called the River Styx when it enters the cave, and finally the name changes again to Cave Creek as it exits the cave.

Portions of the caves are not open to the public because of fossil research. There are at least fifty sites ranging from the Late Pleistocene (126,000 years ago) to the Holocene (9,700 B.C. to the present). The

cave's treasures include portions of a 50,000-year-old fossilized grizzly bear and a jaguar somewhere between 40,000 and 20,000 years old. Rare fossil finds also include mountain beaver and blue grouse. The mammal fossils are of national importance.

The Klamath Siskiyou region is known for its diverse variety of plant and animal life, and its sparse population in some areas support old growth, such as the fir known as "Big Tree." It may be 800 years old, and with its 41-foot (12 m) circumference near the base, it is thought to be the thickest Douglas fir in the state.

Go back in time at the Château at Oregon Caves.

BELOW: *One of southern Oregon's most common—and loudest—birds is the Steller's jay.*

Pacific Northwest Meets Swiss Chalet

Completed in 1934 by local carpenter and self-educated architect Gust Lium, the six-story hotel called The Château is just a few yards from the main entrance to Oregon Caves, is one of the National Parks' Great Lodges, and is listed as a National Historic Landmark. Built as a gift shop and tour guide residence, the hotel now has twenty-three guest rooms, a fine dining room, and a 1930s-style coffee shop.

Using cedar sheathing and other local materials, Lium built his Swiss château with multiple shed and gable roof dormers in the National Park's traditional rustic style that has acquired the nickname "Parkitecture." This style is characterized by employing hand labor, using native wood and stone, blending with the landscape, and rejecting modern buildings' symmetry and regularity. The foundations are the same rock found in the cave. Having very little space to work with, Lium built down instead of out, stacking the back of the chalet down a ravine, where it towers over the creek. Nestled in the mountain, the chalet is truly a way to get away from it all. To the east, the nearest freeway is eighty miles away at Medford, and to the west, the Pacific Coast is ninety miles on an even more roundabout mountain forest route.

More Than a Highway,
It's a Scenic Byway

When is a highway not a highway? When it's the "Volcanic Legacy Scenic Byway All American Road," of course! It is one of only thirty-one All American Roads, known as the crown jewels of the national highway system. A byway is a system of roads combined to cover a broader area than a single highway, and the Volcanic Legacy Scenic Byway follows several roads that surround points of interest along the lower portion of the Cascade Volcanic Arc. You could travel the byway several times and hardly ever take the same road in the same direction twice.

The area included in the byway is five hundred miles long and several hundred miles wide, traveling from volcano to volcano. It begins at Lake Almanor, California, not far from the geothermal activities at Lassen Volcanic National Park. After taking several paths, the byway ends at Crater Lake National Park in Oregon, the highest elevation on the route.

Starting just west of Susanville, one leg of the byway takes you to the northeast of Lassen Volcanic National Park while another road takes you south and west and then north around Lassen Park. From there you travel north sixty miles to McArthur-Burney Falls Memorial State Park. Twenty-seven miles north from the falls, one thousand feet before a roadside café called Bartle Lodge, you can go north on state highway 15 into Lava Beds National Monument, on part of the byway

Unlike most waterfalls in the west, Burney Falls is fed by spring water, so it flows at full force all year long.

system called the Modoc Volcanic Scenic Byway, or west and then north to the city of Mount Shasta. Either route provides excellent views of the giant Mount Shasta volcano.

Both routes join again at the California-Oregon border and lead north to the city of Klamath Falls, north along the western shore of Klamath Lake and the Klamath Lake National Wildlife Refuge, past historic Fort Klamath, and finally up to the south entrance of Crater Lake. It wouldn't be hard to stretch this into a two-week, or even a month-long trip, taking all the roads included in the byway. An excellent map and brochure are available online, or by calling the Volcanic Legacy Scenic Byway headquarters at 1-800-474-2782, or visit their website, www.volcaniclegacybyway.org. But while roads go both ways, rivers almost always flow downhill. The Klamath is the third major river that starts near Crater Lake.

A great egret keeps watch at the Klamath National Wildlife Refuge.

BELOW: *A great blue heron on the lookout.*

Klamath: A Refuge, the Lakes, and the River

More than 50 percent of the Klamath Lakes are filled by the Williamson and Sprague Rivers. To the west, the Wood River also flows into Upper Klamath Lake. It wanders through pine forests and farmlands for eighteen miles and then enters Agency Lake, which connects to Upper Klamath Lake. The land to the east of Agency Lake and on the north shore of Upper Klamath Lake is home to the Upper Klamath National Wildlife Refuge.

The Upper Klamath Wildlife Refuge is mostly for the birds. In 1906, the United States Bureau of Reclamation began the Klamath Project to provide farmland and irrigation water in the Klamath Basin by converting marshland around Upper Klamath Lake and the Klamath River. Farmland was created by making dams and canals that drained Lower Klamath Lake and reduced the size of Tule Lake across the border in California. Recognizing that more and more marshlands were being drained and converted to farmlands, in 1928 the United States Fish and Wildlife Service set aside 15,000 acres (6,070 ha) of open water and freshwater cattail-bulrush marshes as nesting areas for waterfowl and other birds native to the area.

The list of birds is impressive: white pelicans; Canada geese; pintail, mallard, and canvasback ducks; grebes; black terns; great blue herons; great and snowy egrets; and many more. Osprey and eagles nest nearby and fish in the marshlands, and there are beaver dams on the water as well. To ensure seclusion, the refuge is accessible by canoe or kayak only. You can rent canoes nearby, and from the refuge you can see Mount Scott, on the edge of Crater Lake, in the distance.

The Upper Klamath National Wildlife Refuge is administered by the Klamath Basin National Wildlife Refuge Complex at Tulelake, California. And even though Upper Klamath Lake is so close to a bustling city, the adjoining refuge is also home to a wide variety of birds, fish, reptiles, and mammals.

More birds of the region: A prairie falcon at Klamath Wildlife Refuge (ABOVE), *an osprey above the Rogue River* (BELOW), *and a pelican and some ducks at Tule Lake National Wildlife Refuge* (OPPOSITE TOP).

Upper Klamath Lake, sometimes just called Klamath Lake, is twenty-five miles long (40 km) and eight miles wide (13 km). It lies north of the city of Klamath Falls at 4,140 feet (1,260 m). Water levels are managed to protect a fishery and the Klamath River's coho salmon areas south of the lake.

Town residents formed the Linkville Water Ditch Company in 1878 to bring them water from the Link River. Then in 1921, the California Oregon Power Company completed a concrete dam at the south end of Upper Klamath Lake. The dam maintains Klamath Lake water levels, generates hydroelectric power, and provides flood control for the area. It is 22 feet (7 m) high and 435 feet (133 m) long. All the water is channeled down the one-mile-long Link River into Lake Ewauna.

Where Are the Falls in Klamath Falls?

Some call them bull snakes; others call them gopher snakes. Either way, they're one of the most common reptiles along the Oregon–California border.

At least 4,000 years ago, the Klamath and Modoc Indians lived just below the falls at a place they called Yulalona, which means "to move back and forth." Sometimes the water in the Link River would move back up toward the falls, and the natives created rock traps to catch the fish there. But the falls they knew are no longer there because of the Link River Dam.

Judging from historic photographs, the falls were never anything spectacular in the first place. When the lake water narrowed and poured into the Link River, it made a horseshoe-shaped falls with a ten-foot drop.

Settlers arrived near the falls soon after the Applegates blazed their trail through the area. Founded in 1867, the town was originally called Linkville after the Link River, but the name was changed in 1893.

The Southern Pacific Transportation Company arrived in Klamath Falls in 1909 and the town mushroomed overnight from a few hundred residents to several thousand. The lumber industry boomed as dozens of mills were constructed to cut pine and fir.

When the water leaves the Link River Dam, the first one-mile stretch of the Klamath River is known as the Link River because it used to link the Upper and Lower Klamath Lakes. But before the water gets there, it flows over a series of rocks and rapids about a half mile from the dam, and that's all that's left of the original Klamath Falls.

Topsy-Turvy Geography

National Geographic called the Klamath River "a river upside down." It begins on the plains at Klamath Lake, and then flows down into the mountains and to the sea. The Klamath travels 263 miles (423 km) south into California and empties into the Pacific Ocean two miles northwest of the little river town of Klamath, California. The Klamath River and the waters that feed into it include a wide range of landscapes from high desert country where the Williamson and Sprague Rivers feed Upper Klamath and Lower Klamath Lakes, characterized by agricultural areas, grasslands, and wetlands, then down to the lower basin, 15,751 square miles (40,794 sq km) of canyons, forests, and rugged mountains.

Lava Beds National Monument

Ninety miles south of Klamath Falls, Lava Beds National Monument is not only known for lava, but has a large number of caves popular among spelunkers, a wide variety of environmental habitats, and prehistoric rock art dating back five thousand years.

An important part of the Cascade Volcanic Arc, Lava Beds National Monument lies on the north flank of Medicine Lake Volcano. Unlike taller, cone-shaped stratovolcanoes, Medicine Lake is a broad, gently sloped shield-shaped volcano. It was built up over the last half million years by repeated eruptions of a variety of lava types. According to a sign at the Lava Beds Visitor Center, their building was built on top of the Medicine Lake stratovolcano, "the largest volcano in the Cascade Range." Unlike the typical pyramid-shaped volcanoes, Medicine Lake is a "gently sloping accumulation of lava flows measuring 150 miles in diameter and reaching 7,800 feet high. None can match Medicine Lake for sheer volume."

Although the name Lava Beds National Monument brings to mind vast fields of lava chunks, which it has, it is also next to the Tule Lake Wildlife Refuge, a wetlands habitat. The southern part of the monument supports a pine forest because its higher elevation receives more rain and snow than the lower. Going north from there, the land slopes to a juni-

Sagebrush and rock art at Petroglyph Point in Lava Beds National Monument.

Part of a varied conglomeration of Lava Beds inhabitants, this Pacific tree frog rests on some moss.

TOP: *With 5,000 individual carvings on display, Petroglyph Point is one of the largest arrays in the United States.*

per scrubland, and then to lower grasslands and sagebrush.

Sagebrush is an emblem of the American West. Some love it, others hate it, and some after several years become enchanted by the silvery carpet with its gray leaves and pale yellow flower clusters. When he first arrived in Carson City, Nevada, humorist Mark Twain wrote to his mother describing sagebrush: "If you will take a Lilliputian cedar tree for a model, and build a dozen imitations of it with the stiffest article of telegraph wire . . ." you will get an idea of the plant. "When crushed, sagebrush emits an odor which isn't exactly magnolia and equally isn't exactly polecat [skunk] but is a sort of compromise between the two."

The Lava Beds are also home to myriad animal life. Although Pacific tree frogs are usually found along the California Coast, they are just another example of the strange mix of habitats and species found in the monument. The frogs like the water-filled cracks far below the lava flow surface as well as water areas around collapsed caves and entrances.

Geology, geography, and climate are not just factors in biological development but in historic events as well. Napoleon was defeated by the Russian winter, Hannibal conquered the Alps before defeating the Romans, and the Lava Beds were the Modoc Indians' allies.

The Modoc War

From November 29, 1872, until June 1, 1873, the Modocs held out against the U.S. Army's superior numbers and arms. The Modocs lived along the shores of Tule Lake, Lost River, Clear Lake, and Butte Valley in southern Oregon and northern California. Conflicts with European Americans began in 1846, with killings and retaliations on both sides. The U.S. Army moved the Modocs to the Klamath Reservation north of Klamath Lake in 1864, but conditions were bad, with overcrowding, poor supplies, and tension between the Klamath Indians and the Modocs.

Kintpuash, also known as Captain Jack, led his people back to their homelands along the Lost River the following year, asking for a separate reservation there. They were persuaded to return to the reservation, but conditions were still the same. In April of 1870, Captain Jack and 371 Modocs returned to the Lost River. Then on November 28, 1872, Major John Green clashed with them near the Lost River. The Modocs fled by boat across Tule Lake, taking refuge at "Captain Jack's Stronghold," a natural lava rock fortress with deep trenches and small caves at the south end of the lake.

Meanwhile, settlers burned a Modoc village, killing several people. The surviving Indians retaliated later by killing settlers. About 150 Modoc men, women, and children moved to the stronghold. Back at the Klamath Reservation, another 150 who had remained behind left and also joined Captain Jack at the stronghold.

Kintpuash, also known as Captain Jack, led his people in the Modoc Wars to retain their homelands.

BELOW: *A stone circle at Captain Jack's Stronghold in Lava Beds National Monument.*

Skull Cave is one of the largest of more than twenty lava tubes you can explore at Lava Beds.

Three hundred U.S. soldiers attacked the stronghold on January 17, 1873, but the Lava Beds' natural fortification, fog, and extremely cold weather helped the Modocs defeat the army, and many soldiers were killed or wounded, with few losses to the Natives.

Captain Jack continued to ask the government for a reservation on the Lost River, but negotiations broke down and President Ulysses S. Grant appointed a peace commission. A group of Modoc leaders met among themselves on April 11, 1873, and voted to kill the peace commissioners when they met the next day. Captain Jack fought the idea, but was outvoted.

On April 12, Captain Jack's delegation met with the peace commission led by General E.R.S. Canby. Again, Captain Jack asked for a separate reservation and General Canby refused his request. Captain Jack then pulled a revolver and killed the General. The Modoc delegation attacked and other commissioners were wounded.

Conflicts continued, and the Natives were able to elude the Army by traveling through the trenches in the Lava Beds. Finally, Captain Jack surrendered on June 1, 1873. He and two others who attacked the peace commissioners were tried by a military court and hanged at Fort Klamath on October 3, 1873. The Modoc War ended, but for a short while the Lava Beds were the Modocs' allies.

Then, as the twentieth century dawned and men and machines "conquered" the West, even the toughest terrain became less forbidding, more interesting, and even entertaining. The wilderness was less an enemy to be overcome and destroyed than it was a treasure to be preserved and enjoyed.

Local mill worker Judson Howard first visited the Lava Beds in 1916 and returned often over the next twenty years, mapping lava tubes, guiding visitors, and building trails and roads. His letter-writing campaign to the president and Congress helped get national monument designation in 1925.

Judson said, "I found and named 120 caves. I named Sunshine Cave because it is lit up most of the day by sunshine. Catacombs Cave I named for its many branches and alcoves. It made me think of what the burial chambers under Rome might look like. I found it during a blizzard in the winter of 1918." The caves are not the main thing that conjures the past at Lava Beds National Monument, however.

Native Artists Rock the Past

Another claim to fame for Lava Beds is the incredible rock art found in the monument. Ancient art styles can be divided into two methods, those that are pecked into the rock itself (petroglyphs), and those that are painted on the rocks with pigments (pictographs). We are fortunate to have both kinds of rock art at Lava Beds. Some of the art may have been created more than 6,000 years ago.

With 5,000 individual carvings on display, Petroglyph Point is the major "art gallery" at Lava Beds, and probably the largest array anywhere in the United States. According to archaeologists, the artwork on Nightfire Island on the shores of Tule Lake spans a time frame from 5500 B.C. to A.D. 1360.

Because of their perishable nature, the pictographs, painted with charcoal and white clay pigments, are usually found just inside cave entrances, where they are protected from the weather. The best pictographs in the monument are at Symbol Bridge and Big Painted Cave.

While most petroglyph sites in the western United States depict animals, people, and even hands, the Lava Beds images are mostly geometric patterns. One similarity they share with almost every other ancient art gallery, however, is that no one really knows what the symbols mean. Moving south from Lava Beds National Monument, it's fitting that Lassen National Volcanic Park would be at the end of the Volcanic Legacy Scenic Byway. Of all the locations along that set of roads, Lassen has the most current volcanic activity.

The only cave in Lava Beds with artificial lighting, Mushpot Cave's eerie glow hints at how this tube might have looked when the lava was still flowing.

TOP: *No one is quite sure what these petroglyphs mean, but there are a lot more geometric figures here than in other sites around the country.*

Just as Crater Lake is a remnant of Mount Mazama, Brokeoff Mountain is all that is left of the southern flank of Mount Tehama, another long-gone Cascades giant.

BELOW: *Crater Lake and Lassen have a lot in common, including an abundance of golden-mantled ground squirrels.*

Lassen Volcanic National Park

Crater Lake is known for its blue water, and Lava Beds is known for its lava, of course. But Lassen Volcanic National Park is known for its variety of volcanic activity. Here you can find "roaring fumaroles," which are active steam and volcanic-gas vents, the kind that happen before a volcano erupts. There are also pools of boiling water, bubbling and burbling mudpots, and places where steam rises up out of the ground like an overheated car radiator.

The park is named after the 10,457-foot (3,187 m) Lassen Peak, the world's largest plug dome volcano. Dome volcanoes are giant bulges of sticky lava, in this case dacite, that piled up rather than flowing or erupting very far from the vent. The largest of about thirty domes in the area, Lassen formed 27,000 years ago in only a few years.

It is also the southernmost volcano in the Cascade Volcanic Arc, and one of the only places in the world that has all four types of volcanoes—cinder cone, plug dome, shield, and strato—and a wide array of volcanic activity, including fumaroles, mudpots, hot springs, and boiling lakes.

These hydrothermal (hot water) areas are fed by rain and snow runoff that seeps deep underground and is heated by the magma under Lassen Peak. As its name implies, a mudpot, also called a mud pool, is a pool of hot bubbling mud. It is a form of fumarole but with less water. The clay and mud comes from rock that is decomposed by acid and microorganisms in the water. The best examples can be found at Bumpass Hell and Sulphur Works. The largest active area in the park, Bumpass can only be reached by a three-mile round-trip hike, much of it on boardwalks that cover sixteen acres of mudpots, boiling

Geothermal activity abounds on the Devils Kitchen Trail, which takes you past Boiling Springs Lake (TOP) *and Hot Springs Creek* (BOTTOM).

pools, and super-hot steam fumaroles, sounding like a jet engine's roar. At the Sulphur Works, visitors can see mudpots and steam vents right from the sidewalk, no hiking needed. The rangers warn, though, to stay on the trails and walkways! In some places the ground looks solid but you may be stepping onto a thin crust of dirt and fall through into scalding hot mud. Another feature that requires a short hike is Boiling Springs Lake, where water bubbles at 125 degrees Fahrenheit.

According to legend, the Native Americans who lived in the area knew that the peak was full of boiling-hot water and fire and expected it to blow itself apart eventually. Because of its height, immigrants used Lassen Peak as a long-distance locating point. It was named after Peter Lassen, a Danish blacksmith who settled in northern California in the 1830s.

From downtown Red Bluff, California, this ominous view of the Lassen Peak eruption thirty-seven miles away was taken on May 22, 1915.

FLICKR/LASSEN NPS: HISTORIC IMAGE OF LASSEN PEAK ERUPTION PLUME SEEN FROM DOWNTOWN RED BLUFF. BY F.R. ELDREDGE, MAY 22, 1915

A sunset at Summit Lake offers a peaceful respite from Lassen's sulfur pits and boiling fumaroles.

The Last Eruption—Or Is It?

An explosive eruption at the top of Lassen Peak on May 22, 1915, destroyed local areas, and volcanic ash rained down as far as two hundred miles to the east. It was the largest of a series of eruptions from 1914 to 1917 and the most recent until Mount St. Helens in 1980.

Events leading up to the big explosion began with a loud steam-blast explosion on May 30, 1914. More than 180 explosions followed on and off for the next year, blasting a 1,000-foot diameter crater near the top of Lassen Peak. From Manton, California, 40 miles (64 km) away, observers could see glowing blocks of lava tumbling down the sides of the mountain on May 14, 1915. A big black lump of dacite lava filled the crater and spilled out over the edge by the next day. It grew for about six days and then another big steam explosion blasted out another crater nearby. Blocks of lava fell again, but there was no new dome. An avalanche of lava chunks and snow sped three miles an hour (5 kph) down a half-mile-wide path (.8 k) over a low ridge and into Hat Creek. Melting snow and crushed lava created mudflows and then a flood in Hat Creek Valley in the early morning of May 20. That night a more fluid dacite lava flowed 1,000 feet down the sides of Lassen Peak.

After Mount St. Helens' eruption, the United States Geological Survey increased monitoring and is ready to send scientists and monitoring equipment to any location immediately at the sign of increased volcanic activity. In Lassen's case in particular, the National Park Service has an emergency response plan to protect the public against any threat of volcanic eruption.

Go where you may, within a radius of from fifty to a hundred miles or more, there stands before you the colossal cone of Shasta, clad in ice and snow, the one grand, unmistakable landmark—the pole-star of the landscape.

—JOHN MUIR, American poet and naturalist, *Picturesque California*, 1888

Mount Shasta

On a clear day you can see Mount Shasta from Mount Scott next to Crater Lake looming one hundred miles to the south. At 14,179 feet (4,321.8 m) Shasta is the second highest peak in the Cascade Range, the largest stratovolcano in the Cascade Volcanic Arc, and home to seven glaciers.

Shasta is not just one volcano but four overlapping volcanic cones. At 12,330 feet (3,760 m), Shastina is the second largest of the four and is also cone shaped. Although it's considered a satellite of Mount Shasta, it is still the fourth-highest peak in the Cascades.

It all started with andesitic lava eruptions 593,000 years ago that created a stratovolcano on the west side of where Mount Shasta is now. This older volcano's north side collapsed about 340,000 years ago. Today's Mount Shasta grew on top of its predecessor, spewing steam, ash, and lava from four different vents. Each eruption of the four ancestral volcanoes that built Mount Shasta lasted less than a few thousand years, with andesite and dacite domes filling in craters in between the eruptions. Because Shastina still has a crater at the top, geologists say that indicates it erupted less than 10,500 years ago at the end of the last ice age. Since its completion 8,000 years ago with the addition of the fourth and last component, Hotlum Cone, the stratovolcano that we call Mount Shasta erupted every 800 years until 4,500 years ago, when the time span reduced to every 600 years. Fumaroles indicate that there is still volcanic activity there. Meanwhile, thousands of years after Mount Shasta was formed, humans began to live around its base.

An archaeological study found that the prehistoric remains in Shasta Valley date from 8,000 years ago. The people

Mighty Mount Shasta from the shores of Lake Siskiyou.

RIGHT: *The rugged landscape of the Shasta Valley is interspersed with farmland and volcanic cones.*

were hunter-gatherers, whose largest community was around the base of Sheep Rock, just north of Mount Shasta. Their descendants remained until Euro-Americans arrived but never farmed, probably because of frequent droughts.

Mount Shasta is on the Siskiyou Trail, which began as a network of Native American footpaths from California's Central Valley to Oregon's Willamette Valley. The paths became a trail, widened to a road, then a railroad line, and now Interstate 5 follows almost the same course as the Siskiyou Trail.

Two years after Elias Pearce made the first climb to the top in 1854, Harriette Eddy and Mary Campbell McCloud became the first women to reach the top. Responding to a *Yreka Journal* letter claiming that they had been carried to the top, Mrs. Eddy replied, "I was one of the first party of ladies who ever made the ascent of Mount Shasta on September 9, 1856. I can state positively that neither Mrs. Lowery, Mrs. McCloud or myself were 'carried up from the hot sulphur spring to the peak,' or any other portion of the way; and further, the ladies of the party stood the fatigue of the trip full as well as the gentlemen."

Long before America's natural wonders became national parks, Native Americans believed they were spiritual places. People of many faiths believe that the human spirit benefits by communing and harmonizing

Three of the Shasta Valley Wildlife Area's varied inhabitants: an American white pelican (TOP), *a western fence lizard* (ABOVE), *and a western scrub jay* (OPPOSITE).

with these magnificent sites. And when the geography is particularly awesome, metaphysical or alien connections are also attributed to the places. There are those who think there is an alien spaceship base inside the mountain and others who feel that the descendants of the lost continent of Lemuria (also called Mu) live in a village inside Mount Shasta. Whether or not it is a lost continent or an alien outpost, it is definitely a geographic island.

Sky Island

It seems like the plants and animals that live on the upper reaches of Mount Shasta are on an elevated island surrounded by a sea of plains. Species evolved uniquely, and in the second half of the nineteenth century, botanists traveled from all over the world to study the differences. Scottish botanist John Jeffrey named the Jeffrey pine (*Pinus jeffreyi*), John Gill Lemmon named the Shasta red fir (*Abies magnifica* var. *shastensis*), and W. B. Cooke discovered a subspecies of the purple tansy (*Phacelia cookei*), a stemless plant with small purple flowers, which are found only on Mount Shasta. However, twentieth century studies showed that the mountain's plant and animal life is not as diverse as early botanists expected.

In 1898, the U.S. Department of Agriculture's Division of Biology (now the U.S. Department of Fish and Wildlife) sent noted biologist C. Hart Merriam to Mount Shasta. He produced the most comprehensive report on Shasta wildlife, reporting that bighorn sheep, grizzly bears, and elk no longer lived in the area because of disease and predators, including hunters.

The bird list for Mount Shasta is extensive, including but not limited to: chickadees, eagles, hawks, jays, hummingbirds, kinglets, nightjars, nuthatches, tanagers, thrushes, warblers, and woodpeckers. This is also true for mammals, such as bats, black bears, chipmunks, coyotes, mule deer, red foxes, martens, minks, moles, mountain lions, pikas, pronghorn, shrews, skunks, squirrels, and mountain weasels. In his encyclopedic online work, *Mount Shasta: An Annotated Bibliography* created for the College of the Siskiyous, William C. Miesse notes that few studies have been done recently, and that "Mt. Shasta continues to be a habitat for a great wealth of creatures, who perhaps themselves are content in not being disturbed by curious zoologists."

And to celebrate all this natural beauty, hundreds of the world's best artists, such as Albert Bierstadt and Thomas Moran, have created drawings and paintings of Mount Shasta. As the art of photography began to develop, the world's best practitioners, including Carlton Watkins,

Edward Weston, and Ansel Adams, saw Shasta as a perfect subject as well. Writers, poets, and playwrights plied their craft with pen and typewriter too. John Muir, nineteenth-century naturalist and pioneer conservationist, climbed Mount Shasta three times in the 1870s and wrote stories about being trapped in a storm on top of the mountain. The writer Joaquin Miller first achieved his fame in London through his writings about Mount Shasta. The mountain has been their backdrop for a century and a half, and celebrity authors include Rudyard Kipling, Bram Stoker, Robert Louis Stevenson, Mary Austin, Robert Heinlein, and actor Hal Holbrook.

There is no road, café, or gift shop at the top of Mount Shasta; it has not been conquered by bulldozers and bus tours. There is still a silent reverence and a mystery about this place like no other volcano in the Cascades chain.

Land of the Volcanoes

Many times the question has been asked, "How does Crater Lake compare with Yellowstone?" Well, it does not compare at all. As well ask the question, "How does Yosemite compare with the Mammoth Cave?" The scenery is totally different. One may travel through the Alps and see the Yosemite reflected in a thousand forms; so with the Grand Canyon of the Colorado; but Crater Lake stands preeminent and alone, the sole possessor of a peculiar trait of grandeur not matched in all the world.

—WILLIAM GLADSTONE STEEL,
West Shore, March 1886

A Land Before Time

What do all of these places have in common: Crater Lake National Park, Newberry National Volcanic Monument, Oregon Caves National Monument, Lava Beds National Monument, Lassen Volcanic National Park, and Mount Shasta? They are all results of plate tectonics and volcanism thousands or millions of years ago. They are areas set aside for preservation and appreciation by the United States government for its people. Viewing natural wonders gives us perspective, respect for nature, and spiritual connections to forces greater than man. That is true for these stops on the Volcanic Legacy Scenic Byway, an awesome journey through nature's ancient magnificent past. In the 1991 movie *Grand Canyon*, what Danny Glover's character says about the Grand Canyon also applies to the land of the volcanoes:

> "When you sit on the edge of that thing, you just realize what a joke we people are. What big heads we got thinking that what we do is gonna matter all that much. Thinking our time here means diddly to those rocks. It's a split second we been here, the whole lot of us. And one of us? That's a piece of time too small to give a name."